# GREAT THINKING

*The Bridge to Successful Living*

### Finace Bush

Copyright © 2023 Finace Bush
All rights reserved
First Edition

PAGE PUBLISHING
Conneaut Lake, PA

First originally published by Page Publishing 2023

ISBN 979-8-88654-747-4 (pbk)
ISBN 979-8-88654-755-9 (digital)

Printed in the United States of America

*Five percent of the people think; ten percent of the people think they think; and the other eighty-five percent would rather die than think.*
—Thomas A. Edison

*My mission in life is not merely to survive, but to thrive; and to do so with some passion, some compassion, some humor, and some style.*
—Maya Angelou

*Those who fail to think and plan, survive from the wind of the Wings of those who do.*
—Finace Bush Jr.

# Foreword

One of the smartest, most prolific speakers and thinkers I know is Dr. Finace Bush Jr. His ability to take a detailed and confusing thought, idea, or correspondence and simplify it to the most granular proportion for all educational levels to understand is nothing short of astounding.

While Dr. Bush is a highly regarded and well-respected bishop, author, and musician, he is my dear uncle. I have had the blessing of knowing him all my life, quite literally. He served for some time as one of my best, most loving caregivers as one of two of my mom's younger brothers.

From my earliest comprehension, I stood in great awe of "Uncle June" as a man of God—his most remarkable accomplishment. I have been fortunate to establish a professional career around great thinking and building strategies and tactics that align with a company's vision, mission, and goals. Watching Dr. Bush build consensus and understanding with ease and great prowess says a lot about his person. He is both strategic and thoughtful. He possesses the singular ingredient to garner an understanding and a following. He is an outstanding communicator. It is one thing to be a great thinker and collaborator, but one must possess the skill to communicate in a way that even the most basic of thinkers can comprehend the information and thereby exact change.

Dr. Bush walks in the love, light, and presence of God, so his clarity in thoughts comes from living with intention and focus. The book of Ephesians teaches us not to be vague and thoughtless and foolish but be understanding and firmly grasping what the will of the Lord is. This book is so well-written the recipient of this great work will have the blessing of garnering knowledge and understanding within the pages that follow.

It is my hope that you will read this and be as richly informed as I was. This book provides a pathway and technique that can be used for your individual success. I hope it serves as a guide for you to understand your potential, as it did me.

It is also my prayer that you will use this as a tool to discover your personal brand and identity.

May God add a blessing to you and this word. Praying for your daily renewal with love.

Adrienne R. Fairwell, APR

*****

In 1998, shortly after rededicating my life to Christ, I heard a message that continues to resound in my subconscious daily. The title of the message was "Think about What You Are Thinking About." I don't recall the preacher who delivered the message. I don't recall the church where I heard it from, but realizing the concept of metacognition has been life-changing for me. Before hearing that sermon, I had never considered that my thought life could be managed. I now understand the power and responsibility to be intentional about my thought life.

Today, as I sit under the tutelage of my pastor, Dr. Finace Bush Jr., at Crown Kingdom Cultural Center, I am learning to walk out godly principles that frequently guide me into self-assessment as I learn to apply the Word of God to my everyday decisions. Great Thinkers Academy offers readers the opportunity to think deeply about the importance of choosing to think. The literature brings to light the often overlooked option to use our God-given ability to imagine a better tomorrow.

In this current age when artificial intelligence is used so casually on our smartphones, in our cars, to monitor our health workouts, and even to play music from our kitchen countertops, we are inundated with suggestions of what to think. Our preferences and patterns of behavior are systematically exploited via marketing algorithms. Pop-up ads and seemingly random images come to us courtesy of well-funded, highly calculated marketing plans. Distractions are strategically placed in our view and in our hearing. These interesting distractions are cancerous to purpose; and the result is wasted time, effort, and brain power, which lead to untapped personal development and unrealized potential, which is ultimately taken to the grave.

When we focus on what is trending, we begin to seek external guidance for how we manage our thought life. Celebrity news and political views can replace what God designed the Holy Spirit to do in our lives. As Christians, we have the responsibility to seek to understand God's plans and purpose for your time and talent.

What if we consciously chose to live by the instructions Paul gave to the church at Philippi in Greece? He advised them to *think*, saying, "Finally, brothers and sisters, whatever is true, whatever is noble, whatever is right, whatever is pure, whatever is lovely, whatever is admirable—if anything is excellent or praiseworthy—think about such things" (Philippians 4:8 NIV).

He encouraged the people of Philippi to be selective in choosing what to think upon.

Imagine if you chose to discover what God has gifted to you inside your own mind. Imagine what you can create when you allow your thoughts to explore new possibilities and unique solutions. Imagine you living out your life as a great thinker—the possibilities are legendary!

Trina Brinson

*****

This book is written by a young minister and artist that I have had the pleasure of knowing since his birth. You see, I am the elder sister of Dr. Bishop Finace Bush Jr. from New Ellenton, South Carolina, in Aiken County.

I am very honored to have had the pleasure of watching him grow from a curious little fellow—who was always concerned about "thus said the Lord"—to the most esteemed minister that I know. His interest and dedication to God has been his life's journey. He is very clairvoyant of his personal accounts of his journey in life to his spiritual growth and his dedication to gain knowledge of God's Word and how to apply it to his life to not only strive but to thrive.

The book that you are about to read is very insightful. It conveys a variety of Finace's personal accounts of his unique journey called life and how his faith in God's *promises* has brought him through. Like many other great thinkers before him, who left great marks on the world, he shows us how he used his big imagination to think and plan his way to the successful life he now enjoys.

I pray that you find this book written by Dr. Bishop Finace Bush Jr. as insightful and enjoyable as I have.

Blessings and love.

Rhonda Bush Johnson

This book is about game changers and force multipliers who find ways through thinking to leave their prints on society regardless of odds and statistics.

# Introduction

The world needs more great thinkers, especially in this most transitional dispensation of our time and existence. Since the World Health Organization declared the coronavirus a pandemic a little more than two years ago, new Yelp data showed nearly a half million businesses opened in America during that time, an optimistic sign of the state of the US economic recovery. Between March 11, 2020, and March 1, 2021, Yelp has seen more than 487,500 new business listings on its platform in the United States. More than 15 percent of the new entities were restaurant and food businesses. Of the almost half million new businesses that have opened, about 59 percent were within the "professional, local, home, and auto" category on Yelp.

"The number of new business openings—particularly the high number of new home, local, professional, and auto-services businesses—also shows great potential for those industries in the future," said Justin Norman, vice president of data science at Yelp.

While it is a great time to be born because of the multifarious opportunities available in today's society, it's ironic that the challenge to succeed has become more difficult because of a variety of contributing factors. One of my most frequent sayings during lectures and motivational speeches on self-awareness is that "life can be highly consumptive with its daily demands for existence, and that's without the unanticipated challenges that occur so frequently."

Although we are constantly challenged in this age to make a living and acquire means to survive, like Maya Angelou suggested, our mission must be to thrive rather than merely survive, which will require a great deal of thinking and planning from day to day, especially if you, as an individual, will do so with passion, compassion, humor, and style.

Pastoring a multicultural church gives me the opportunity to meet diverse kinds of men and women who are looking to God for assistance and breakthroughs in different areas of their lives. Some of these people are spiritual, traditional, or religious. Some are professional, gifted, savvy, witty, loving, cautious, free-spirited, motivated, talented, and highly skilled. Yet others are friendly, sociable, and great for networking and connecting with people. *What* is clear to me is that regardless of who these individuals are and how they struggle in their personal lives, those who are willing to *think* through their challenges, whether classified as carnal or spiritual, godly or ungodly, find insightful ways to overcome their challenges rather than looking to someone else to solve them. They discover that a *bridge* to successful, wholesome living is *thinking*. This process requires spending time with the things God is trying to reveal to you through your mind to stimulate your *imagination*.

It is apparent that those who are ready to think are usually those who will most likely succeed because they will include God's wisdom and take responsibility for their own lives. This is regardless of their spiritual status, race, gender, class, or color.

Every day I encounter young adults who are already at their wits' end, struggling with the perplexities of a life they're trying to construct for themselves without much deliberation or consideration. One reason Ecclesiastes 12:1 said, "Remember now your Creator in the days of your youth, Before the difficult days come, And the years draw near when you say, 'I have no pleasure in them,'" was to convey an antidote against the diseases of youth, the excessive love of amusement, and the wrong indulgence of sensual pleasures, which are vanities all children and youths are subject to.

Unaware of the sleeping giant within, I often ask youths and young adults what their goals are or if they have a life plan in place to assist them in knowing what's next. The most frequent response I get is "I, or we, are so busy between work, children, and household demands that we don't have time to *think*." And every single time I hear this response, I remember that Thomas Edison said, "Five percent of the people *think*; ten percent of the people think they *think*; and the other eighty-five percent would rather *die* than *think*."

In order to change this self-perpetuating cycle of insanity, weariness, and struggle, a great deal of intentional, strategic, and big-picture thinking is necessary. Good, healthy thoughts manufacture revenue, create a wide range of opportunities, and foster activities that generate a healthy lifestyle.

*Time* allotted for thinking and listening to your spirit is actually more important than the things that continually consume your time each day, leaving you weary, frustrated, and spent. In fact, if you don't begin to incorporate *time* to think and plan your life, it is likely going to get worse. As the saying goes, "those who fail to plan, plan to fail."

*If you do what you've always done, you will get what you always got. If you want something different, you must do something different. To do something different requires new information, consideration, and determination!*

Mr. Capes, a senior real estate agent who's a great friend of mine, once pointed out to me that when he was growing up, a lot of his family's time, alongside many other families throughout the communities of our world, was wasted because of an imperceptible adversary he identified in this scenario titled "Met a Stranger."

## Met a Stranger

A few years after I was born, my dad met a stranger who was new to our small town.

From the beginning, Dad was fascinated with this enchanting newcomer and soon invited him to live with our family.

The stranger was quickly accepted and was around from then on.

As I grew up, I never questioned his place in my family. In my young mind, he had a special niche. My parents were complementary instructors. Mom taught me good from evil, and Dad taught me to obey.

But the stranger was our storyteller.

He would keep us spellbound for hours on end with adventures, mysteries, and comedies.

If I wanted to know anything about politics, history, or science, he always knew the answers about the past, understood the present, and even seemed able to predict the future!

He took my family to the first major-league ball game. He made me laugh, and he made me cry.

The stranger never stopped talking, but Dad didn't seem to mind.

Sometimes, Mom would get up quietly while the rest of us were shushing one another to listen to what he had to say, and she would go to the kitchen for peace and quiet.

(I wonder now if she ever prayed for the stranger to leave.)

Dad ruled our household with certain moral convictions, but the stranger never felt obligated to honor them.

Profanity, for example, was not allowed in our home—not from us, our friends, or any visitors.

Our longtime visitor, however, got away with four-letter words that burned my ears and made my dad squirm and my mother blush.

My dad didn't permit the liberal use of alcohol, but the stranger encouraged us to try it on a regular basis.

He made cigarettes look cool, cigars manly, and pipes distinguished.

He talked freely (much too freely!) about sex. His comments were sometimes blatant, sometimes suggestive, and generally embarrassing.

I now know that my early concepts about relationships were influenced strongly by the stranger.

Time after time, he opposed the values of my parents, yet he was seldom rebuked—and *never* asked to leave.

More than fifty years have passed since the stranger moved in with our family.

He has blended right in and is not nearly as fascinating as he was at first. Still, if you could walk into my parents' den today, you would still find him sitting over in his corner, waiting for someone to listen to him talk and watch him draw his pictures.

# GREAT THINKING

His name?
We just call him "TV."
He has a wife now—we call her "Computer."
Their first child is "Cell Phone."
Second child is "iPod."
And *just born a few years ago* was his grandchild: "iPad."

It was important to unveil this diabolical and imperceptible adversary because so many who need to explore the possibility of a purposeful life are captured either by the spell of Television or his offspring. Only the correct use of these mediums will allow them to become formidable allies that can give rise to valuable information exchanges.

Albert Einstein once stated that "thinking is hard work; that's why so few do it." For this reason, my hope is that as you read this book, you will be challenged to become one of the world's great thinkers.

# The *Power* to *Succeed* is in *You*

*Ye are of God, little children, and have overcome them: because greater is he that is in you, than he that is in the world.*
—1 John 4:4 (KJV)

Have you ever considered the potential of creativity that abides in you as a thinker or thinking agency? Even more, if you have accepted Christ, the Son of God, as your Savior, do you have any idea how enhanced the capacity of your potential has expanded?

Let me encourage you to read the four Gospels and study the methods Jesus demonstrated when faced with limitations, oppositions, and adventurous challenges through faith in an unrestricted imagination. Such an imagination is the liberated ability to think freely, without imposed restrictions and limitations, while exploring and embracing opportunities only yielded to those daring to go where only a few are willing to explore.

If you are "born-again," you are born of God, and the same "greater One" now lives inside of you.

This is vitally important because to use faith as Jesus did gives you the ability to imagine like Him and communicate with the invisible forces that still exist in the heavenly realm, which is the apostle Paul's purpose for encouraging us to urgently renew our *minds* as we live and walk by faith.

Today it is becoming increasingly clear that the advancement of technology (the application of scientific knowledge for practical purposes) is the combination between what's in a man's head and what's in his hand.

In this, the increase of man's knowledge, as Daniel prophesied, is removing impossibilities as in the days of Babel—the period mentioned in Genesis 11, wherein man moved to prove his ability to tower himself to God's throne without His assistance.

A scene that brings us back to God's original intent before man's imagination became distorted by Satan with "only evil continually." I say this because I believe, according to the Holy Scriptures, that God is bringing the society back to His *image*, divinely implanting Himself in man's imagination. This is consistent with Hebrews 10:16 (AMP): "This is the covenant that I will make with them After those days, says the Lord: I will imprint My laws upon their heart, And on their mind I will inscribe them [producing an inward change]."

So where did man get this ability to duplicate or become an affront to God, his Creator? And what about man gave him the potential to function as such high-level achievers? At Babel, they cast their aspersions while joining their mental faculties by speaking harmonic words to expand their capacity to think themselves into a unified imagination so potent that only God Himself could stop.

Somehow they realized that *originally*, "*man* was *a* made *image*." In this, man was "made to *imagine*," and ultimately man was "made to create by his *imagination*." Or we could say in the *likeness* of his Creator, *man* finds or discovers his true *image*.

Here, both flesh and spirit, heaven and earth, was to be put together in *man* because he was created to be unified and in alliance with both worlds.

This means that God's *image* upon man consists of three things:

1. In his nature and constitution
2. In his place and authority
3. In his purity and rectitude

In his nature and constitution: not those of his body (because God does not have a body) but those of his *soul*. It is the *soul* of man that actually bears, carries, and exhibits God's *image*. The *soul* is a spirit—an intelligent, immortal, influencing, active spirit—herein resembling God, the Father of spirits and the soul of the world. "The *spirit* of man is the candle of the Lord." The soul of man, considered in its three noble faculties—understanding, will, and active power—is perhaps the brightest, clearest looking glass in nature wherein to see God.

In his place and authority: "Let us make man in our image, and let him have dominion." Man is God's representative, or viceroy, upon earth as he has the government of the inferior creatures because they are not capable of fearing and serving God; therefore, God has appointed them to fear and serve man. Yet man's government of himself by the freedom of his will has in it more of God's image than his government of the creatures.

In his purity and rectitude: God's image upon man consists of knowledge, righteousness, and true holiness. Notice that Ephesians 4:24 AMP says, "And put on the new self [the regenerated and renewed nature], created in God's image, [godlike] in the righteousness and holiness of the truth [living in a way that expresses to God your gratitude for your salvation]." Colossians 3:10 AMP says, "And have put on the new [spiritual] self who is being continually renewed in true knowledge in the image of Him who created the new self." This is important because originally, man's understanding allowed him to see divine things clearly, and there were no errors nor mistakes in his knowledge. However, Solomon declares in Ecclesiastes 7:29, "Behold, I have found only this [as a reason]: God made man upright and uncorrupted, but they [both men and women] have sought out many devices [for evil]." His will complied readily and universally with the will of God, without reluctance or resistance. His affections were all regular, and he had no inordinate appetites or passions. His thoughts were easily brought and fixed to the best subjects, and there was no vanity nor ungovernableness in them. All the inferior powers were subject to the dictates and directions of the superior without any mutiny or rebellion. Initially, our first parents were both holy and happy in having the *image* of God upon them. *Notice* Genesis 1:26–28:

> And God said, "Let us make man in our image, after our likeness: and let them have dominion over the fish of the sea, and over the

fowl of the air, and over the cattle, and over all the earth, and over every creeping thing that creeps upon the earth." So God created man in his own *image*, in the *image* of God created he him; male and female created he them. And God blessed them, and God said unto them, "Be fruitful, and multiply, and replenish the earth, and subdue it: and "have" dominion over the fish of the sea, and over the fowl of the air, and over every living thing that moves upon the earth.

Here we see that those who imagine like Him will speak like Him as Adam in Genesis 2. Notice:

So the Lord God formed out of the ground every animal of the field and every bird of the air, and brought them to Adam to see what he would *call* them; and whatever the man *called* a living creature, that was its name. And the man gave names to all the livestock, and to the birds of the air, and to every animal of the field; but for Adam there was not found a helper [that was] suitable (a companion) for him. (Genesis 2:19–20 AMP)

The problem we face today is as it was in the days of Moses when the ten spies brought back an evil report. The wrong spies have brought back a dual and divisive message to the church that has distorted the ability of many in the church to *perceive wholistically* and *imagine unrestrictedly* as sons of God.

*Point is*, today it is actually better for a man to have an unrestricted flourishing imagination with limited intellectual knowledge than to have divisive intellectual knowledge that restricts his *imagination*.

Why? Because a flourishing imagination is the transference of God's consciousness into the spiritual *mind* of man.

# GREAT THINKING

Our adversary, the devil, knows that to influence man's thought life is to infect his imagination and ultimately distort man's creative genius. And this is primarily because the principle of Proverbs 23:7 says, "For as he thinks in his heart, so is he."

Lucifer's diabolical strategy was to tease man's imagination in order to provoke or initiate his lust for that which was forbidden.

In the Genesis 3:5–7 account, the adversary triggered Eve's inquisitiveness by using loaded words designed to deceive. He imposed his logic by saying, "For God knows that on the day you eat from the tree your eyes will be opened [that is, you will have greater awareness], and you will be like God, knowing [the difference between] good and evil."

Verse 6 and 7 say,

> And when the woman *saw* [imagined or viewed herself apart from God's words] that the tree was good for food, and that it was delightful to look at, and a tree to be desired in order to make one wise and insightful, she took some of its fruit and ate it; and she also gave some to her husband with her, and he ate.
>
> *Then* the eyes of the two of them were opened [that is, their awareness increased], and *they knew* that they were naked; and *they* fastened fig leaves together and *made* themselves *coverings*.

Historically, man's imagination has gone through a serious digression and divergence since this fall in Genesis 3.

We've discovered three things from this account:

1. *To alter what one imagines is to alter their ability to fulfill the original purpose for which they were created.*
2. *Lucifer knew man's potential to duplicate God was in his ability to "imagine" like God.*
3. *When the influencing source becomes the "self," the privilege of God's power is compromised, and our seed is also corrupted.*

Notice the immediate impact of this corruption upon the *seed* of Adam and Eve in Genesis 4:4–8 (AMP):

> But Abel brought [an offering of] the [finest] firstborn of his flock and the fat portions. And the Lord had respect (regard) for Abel and for his offering; but for Cain and his offering He had no respect. So Cain became extremely angry (indignant), and he looked annoyed and hostile.
>
> And the Lord said to Cain, "Why are you so angry? And why do you look annoyed? If you do well [believing Me and doing what is acceptable and pleasing to Me], will you not be accepted? And if you do not do well [but ignore My instruction], sin crouches at your door; its desire is for you [to overpower you], but you must master it."
>
> Cain talked with Abel his brother [about what God had said]. And when they were [alone, working] in the field, Cain attacked Abel his brother and killed him.

Next, their *seed* became the catalyst for social corruption.

*When the image of our seed is compromised, society becomes infiltrated with altered defective manifestations. This sheds light on Genesis 6:3:*

> And the Lord said, "My spirit shall not always strive with man, for that he also is flesh: yet his days shall be a hundred and twenty years."

*Verses 5 and 6 affirms "why."*

> The Lord saw that the wickedness (depravity) of man was great on the earth, and that every imagination or intent of the *thoughts* of his heart were only evil continually.

> The Lord regretted that He had made mankind on the earth, and He was [deeply] grieved in His heart.

## *Three important observations*

1. Wrong imagination constitutes *unrighteous alignment.*
2. Wisdom says, "Guard you heart diligently from misaligned imaginations" (Proverbs 4:23).
3. Your *capacity* to *see* is your *ability* to *be* a reflection of the *image* of God!

The widespread corruption through man's imagination became the dominant influence among social leaders.

*Reliance upon the self apart from dependence upon God becomes an adopted agreement by social leaders.*

*Notice* that Genesis 11:1–8 says,

> Now the whole earth spoke one language and used the same words (vocabulary). And as people journeyed eastward, they found a plain in the land of Shinar and they settled there. They said one to another, "Come, let us make bricks and fire them thoroughly [in a kiln, to harden and strengthen them]." So they used brick for stone [as building material], and they used tar (bitumen, asphalt) for mortar. They said, "Come, let us build a city for ourselves, and a tower whose top will reach into the heavens, and let us make a [famous] name for ourselves, so that we will not be scattered [into separate groups] and be dispersed over the surface of the entire earth [as the Lord instructed]."
>
> And the Lord said, "Behold, they are *one* [unified] people, and they all have the same *language*. This is only the beginning of what they

> will do [in rebellion against Me], and now no evil *thing* they *imagine* they can do will be impossible for them." [Notice the emphasis—nothing *restrained* that they have *imagined* themselves doing. Now the Lord came down to see the city and the tower that the sons of men had built.] Come, let Us (Father, Son, Holy Spirit) go down and there confuse and mix up their language, so that they will not understand one another's speech. So the Lord scattered them abroad from there over the surface of the entire earth; and they stopped building the city.

It's important to remember that after Babel, man went through a period wherein he either had knowledge but lacked the ability to perform it, or he had ability but lacked knowledge for proper applications.

*To reset the social stratum of an infected world, God called Abraham, the father of faith!*

*Notice* that Abraham, in Genesis 12, was called to reintroduce society to the correct use of man's imagination directed by *faith* in God. It is clear that Abraham struggled initially, although he eventually grasped it.

God allowed Abraham to demonstrate to us the complications of having a distorted use of the mind and the detriment of an imagination that could not easily embrace the *power* of *belief* in a promise from God.

> Now [in Haran] the Lord *had said* to Abram, "Go away from your country, And from your relatives And from your father's house, To the land which I will show you." (Genesis 12:1 AMP)

Although it took a significant amount of time, eventually Abraham was able to grasp the understanding of God's will for him. Truly "faith comes by hearing."

# GREAT THINKING

Today, after centuries have passed, we are fulfilling a prophetic era regarding the increase of knowledge that speaks again to the *power* of *imagination* used righteously, wherein whatever a man can *imagine* in his heart, he can *manufacture* with his hands. I refer to this as the *advancement of technology*.

Daniel 12:1–4 says that "knowledge will increase." Notice:

> Now at that time Michael, the great prince who stands guard over the sons of your people, will arise. And there will be a time of distress such as never occurred since there was a nation until that time; and at that time your people, everyone who is found written in the book, will be rescued. And many of those who sleep in the dust of the ground will awake, these to everlasting life, but the others to disgrace and everlasting contempt. And those who have *insight* will shine like the glow of the expanse of heaven, and those who *lead* the many to righteousness, like the stars forever and ever. But as for you, Daniel, keep these words secret and seal up the book until the end of time; many will roam about, and *knowledge* will *increase*. (Daniel 12:1–4)

*Although knowledge continues to increase, the imagination of many has become Satan's avenue to societal corruption.*

*Let's read* Isaiah 55:7–11 because here the prophet cries,

> Let the wicked leave (behind) his way And the unrighteous man his thoughts; And let him return to the Lord, And He will have compassion (mercy) on him, And to our God, For He will abundantly pardon.
>
> "For My *thoughts* are not your thoughts, Nor are your *ways* My ways," declares the Lord.

"For as the heavens are higher than the earth, So are My ways higher than your ways And My *thoughts* higher than your thoughts. For as the rain and snow come down from heaven, And do not return there without watering the earth, Making it bear and sprout, And providing seed to the sower and bread to the eater.

So will My word be which goes out of My mouth; It will not return to Me *void* (useless, without result), Without accomplishing what I desire, And without succeeding in the matter for which I sent it."

*Also*, Romans 8:4–8 emphasizes

That the [righteous and just] requirement of the Law might be fulfilled in us who do not live our lives in the ways of the flesh [guided by worldliness and our sinful nature], but [live our lives] in the ways of the Spirit [guided by His power].

For those who are living according to the flesh set their *minds* on the things of the flesh [which gratify the body], but those who are living according to the Spirit, [set their *minds* on] the things of the Spirit [His will and purpose].

Now the *mind* of the flesh is death [both now and forever—because it pursues sin]; but the *mind* of the Spirit is life and peace [the spiritual well-being that comes from walking with God—both now and forever];

The *mind* of the flesh [with its sinful pursuits] is actively hostile to God. It does not submit itself to God's law, since it cannot, and those who are in the flesh [living a life that caters to sinful appetites and impulses] cannot please God."

# Many Rewarded for Great Thinking

Early proof that the innate power to succeed is inside and can be discovered if you're willing to cautiously consider your life's challenges was recently revealed during my visit to the East Coast.

While visiting several tourist sites in Beaufort, South Carolina, the tour guide provided an insightful historical account about an enslaved African American born on April 5, 1839, named Robert Smalls, who is revered as a great strategic thinker. He escaped to freedom in a Confederate supply ship and eventually became a sea captain for the Union Navy. Although Smalls was born to a house slave, Lydia Polite, and was raised in the McKee house, he enjoyed a little more acceptance in the community.

When Smalls was twelve, the McKee family moved to Charleston, where Smalls was hired as a day laborer on the waterfront, working as a rigger and eventually a sailor. In 1856, he married Hannah Jones, a slave hotel maid who worked in Charleston.

## *Gunboat deckhand*

At the outbreak of the Civil War in March 1861, Smalls was hired as a deckhand on the Confederate supply ship, the *Planter*, a converted cotton steamer that carried supplies between forts in Charleston Harbor.

## *Strategic thinking*

Over the course of several months, Smalls learned all he could about navigating the ship and waited for an opportunity to escape.

In the predawn hours of May 13, 1862, while the White officers and crew slept in Charleston, Smalls and a crew of eight men, along with five women and three children (including Smalls's wife and two children), quietly slipped the *Planter* out of Charleston Harbor, a daring escape that took indomitable, lionhearted courage.

Over the next few hours, Smalls successfully navigated the ship through five checkpoints, offering the correct signal to pass each, and then headed out to open waters and the Union blockade. It was daring and dangerous, and if caught, the crew was prepared to blow up the vessel.

The startled crew of the USS *Onward*, the first ship in the blockade to spot the *Planter*, almost fired on it before Smalls had the Confederate flag struck and raised a white bedsheet, signaling surrender. The ship's treasure of guns, ammunition, and important documents proved to be a wealth of information, telling the Union commanders of shipping routes, mine locations, and the times that Confederate ships docked and departed.

## *Wartime hero and spokesperson*

The story of the courageous escape of Robert Smalls became a national phenomenon and was one of the factors encouraging President Abraham Lincoln to authorize free African Americans to serve in the Union military. Congress bestowed a $1,500 cash prize on Smalls, and he went on a speaking tour, recounting his heroics and recruiting African Americans to serve in the Union Army. During the rest of the war, Smalls balanced his role as a spokesperson and Union Navy captain on the *Planter* and the ironclad USS *Keokuk*, conducting seventeen missions in and around Charleston.

Before dismissing the group from the tour, with a deep sigh, clearly in appreciation of this historic account, the guide declared, "I pray this information will inspire and provoke some of you to use your God-given gift of *thinking* to free your families from mediocrity and purposeless living."

A grandfather of ten, I find myself constantly reminding my grandchildren, who are millennials, to put aside their gadgets and spend quality time in thinking exercises, reading, competitive activities, and challenging games to continually exercise their minds. It is vitally important to me that they learn how to effectively hear and discern God's voice within and to think and navigate through life's challenges as they surface without becoming overwhelmed, also that they learn how to think relatively, situationally, and creatively about the future they aspire to experience.

I think it interesting that the wisdom of God instructs parents to "train up children" during their age of vanity to keep them from the sins and snares of it, especially while in their learning age, in order to prepare them for what they are destined to become.

It's important to catechize children in order to initiate them, which requires keeping them under discipline. The implication is to *train* them as soldiers, who are taught to handle their arms, keep rank, and observe the word of command.

*Train them up* not in the way they would go because the bias of their corrupt hearts would draw them away from their purpose but in the way they should go—the way in which, if you love them, you would have them go.

In this, through close observation and constant follow-up, the child is trained up according to their potential, capacity, ability, and interest with a gentle but firm hand like nurses feeding children little and often.

An obvious reason many adults have lived frustrated practically all of their lives is because they missed appropriate training during their youth. Many at a young age were pressured by their parents and peers to go job hunting instead of emphasizing the importance of exploring and learning how to think and meditate by listening to their spirit. There was little to no pressure or instructions to use their minds, influenced by their desires, to shape and assume responsibility for the life they aspired to live. In fact, many grew up without ever being instructed to pray and seek God for personal vision with specific plans for their existence, which was a tremendous oversight because to prioritize looking for a job without appropriate thinking exercises and training subjects you to the ideas, ideals, or systems of others. And this is detrimental, especially if you haven't given yourself an opportunity to see how well you will perform by working within the parameters of your own personal interest, ability, and capacity, which enables you to live in a way that corresponds with your own personal vision and dreams. I'm talking here about maximizing your personal life.

That's right. Each of us have inside of us an innate ability to function on a godly level that will exceed anything we've accomplished without it.

God has tailored an *anointing* specifically for you. It's unique to you, fits no one but you, and is the epitome of your essence. This anointing is your God-given right to gain maximum functional fulfillment and peace both naturally and spiritually. Think about it, and imagine yourself living daily in a way that gives you maximum functional fulfillment and peace. You can do it. It's possible!

Although financial gain is not my first requisite for this wholesome living that yields personal fulfillment, understanding the importance of gaining personal concept-ability through personal interest can assist you individually in acquiring early financial success.

Journalist John Boitnott, in listing "40 Young People Who Became Millionaires before They Were 20," stated, "It is often awe-inspiring to think about how early some of the world's most famous entrepreneurs got their start. Many of them simply had a fantastic *idea* and then just worked their butts off to make it reality." I listed a few of these young inspired *thinkers* to motivate you to *think* about the possibility of carving out your own avenue to acquire financial stability and succeed early.

Tyler Dikman—by eighth grade, Dikman was charging $15 an hour to fix computers. His skills caught the eye of Merrill Lynch executives, and he was hired by Malcolm Taaffe at age fifteen. He soon started his own business, Cooltronics, repairing computers—making millions and scoring him a spot on *Businessweek*'s "25 under 25" list.

Juliath Brindak—she began creating sketched characters at age ten and then developed a complementary social media platform at sixteen. Her Miss O & Friends company is now worth an estimated $15 million, though Brindak gets most of her revenue from ads.

# GREAT THINKING

David and Catherine Cook—this brother-and-sister team got rich by creating MyYearbook.com, which remains a player in the social media realm. Their older brother invested $250,000 in their digital yearbook idea, and today the site is worth about $100 million.

John Magennis—starting a web design business at fourteen, Magennis is totally self-taught. Initially, he charged just $15 per site, but today he can demand upward of $30,000 per site. He earned his first million by his sixteenth birthday.

Mark Zuckerberg—many people forget that when Facebook's founder started swimming in wealth, he was a young college student. Almost everyone knows the story of Facebook, and Zuckerberg's now one of the wealthiest people in the world at around $20 billion, regardless of age.

To repeat John Boitnott, journalist and digital consultant,

> It's hard not to feel a bit competitive after reading about all these young entrepreneurs. However, try to take away at least this one important lesson from the list. It's never too late—or early—to chase your dreams. Anything can happen with a great idea, hard work, and creativity. These teens are living proof.

I highlighted his takeaway point to emphasize the importance of pursuing your God-given dreams because they contain the seeds of individual success.

Wise man Solomon once stated, "The blessing of the Lord makes one rich without adding sorrow." In this, God has provided a pathway for each of us to succeed at being who we were designed to be and doing what He purposed us to do. His way to success unveils more than a wealth in finances; it yields peace that brings personal fulfillment.

With the assistance of good parenting and the guidance of principal persons, you must be taught and trained to become a good manager and steward over what God has invested in you. Throughout your life's journey, you will be asked, *What* will you do with your time, talents, and treasures? I call them the three *T*s of your "life's potential."

Each day I awake on planet Earth, God affords me two brand-new privileges—time and choice!

The way I value and use these two resources ultimately determines the nature of the third gift—the one I give to myself, which is chance!

The late Dr. Myles Munroe said, "I am convinced that our Creator never intended for us to be normal—that is, to get lost in the crowd of the norm."

This is evidenced by the fact that among the 5.8 billion people on this planet, no two individuals are alike; their fingerprints, genetic code, and chromosome combinations are all distinct and unique.

*He went on to say,*

> In reality, God created all people to be originals, but we continue to become copies of others. Too often we are so preoccupied with trying to fit in, that we never stand out. You were designed to be distinctive, special, irreplaceable, and unique, so refuse to be "normal"! Go beyond average! Do not strive to be accepted, rather strive to be yourself. Shun the minimum; pursue the maximum. Utilize all your functions and maximize yourself!

He concluded by saying, "Use yourself up for the glory of your Creator. I admonish you: Die empty. Die fulfilled by dying unfilled."

I place tremendous emphasis on this statement because *God wants you to remember His* special care, His special design, and His special investments in *you.*

The psalmist David once said,

> You are the one who put me together inside my mother's body. How *precious* also are Your *thoughts* to *me*, O God! How *great* is the sum of them! If I should count them, they would be

more in number than the sand; When I awake, I
am still with You. (Psalm 139:13, 17–18)

You must understand that *everyone created by God was given purpose in the form of unique gifts*. My emphasis is that each of us were fearfully and wonderfully made, which means there is a unique, creative purpose for which we all were born.

Jeremiah, the prophet, is a good example of God's unique design and purpose for each of us—his early designation to the work and office of a prophet, which God gives him notice of as a reason for his early application to that business. His prophetic book states that the Word of the Lord came to him with a satisfying assurance that it was the Word of the Lord and not a delusion.

Herein, God told him that He had ordained him to be a prophet to the nations—not to the Jews only but also to the neighboring nations. He explained to him that before he was born, even in His eternal counsel, He had designed Jeremiah to be a prophet. God also let him know that He who gave him his commission is the same that gave him his being. He formed him in the belly and brought him forth out of the womb; therefore, He was his rightful owner and could employ him and make use of him as He pleased.

This commission was given to him in pursuance of the purpose God had purposed in himself concerning him before he was born.

Notice: "I knew thee, and I sanctified thee"—in other words, "I determined that you should be a prophet and set you apart for that office."

Paul, the apostle, also said of himself throughout his writings that God had separated him from his mother's womb to be an apostle, which makes it clear that our great Creator knows what use to make of every man before He makes him. The Scriptures declare, "He has made all for himself, and of the same lumps of clay designs a vessel of honor or dishonor, as He pleases" (Romans 9:21).

What God has designed men, for He will call them to. His purposes cannot be frustrated. It is original endowment, not education, that makes a prophet.

*See* Genesis 12:1–6, Exodus 3:3–14, Jeremiah 1:4–8, Luke 1:26–38.

Discovering your personal identity and the purpose you were born is first *priority*. For this reason, God has provided gifted parents and principal persons to assist you in *becoming* you!

The years of the life of Moses are remarkably divided into three forties: the first forty he spent as a prince in Pharaoh's court, the second as a shepherd in Midian, the third a king in Jeshurun.

Moses had finished his second forty when he received his commission to bring Israel out of Egypt. He was born to be Israel's deliverer, and yet not a word is said of it to him till he is eighty years of age.

He was keeping the flock (tending sheep) near mount Horeb. This was a poor employment for a man of his education, yet he was satisfied with it because through this employment, he learned meekness and contentment to a high degree.

God will encourage industry. Even the shepherds were keeping their flocks when they received the tidings of our Savior's birth. Satan loves to find us idle, but God is well-pleased when He finds us employed.

The problem is that whenever you solicit a job at random without a plan or specific purpose, it's important to consider how it will impact your freedom to be available for the accomplishment of your dreams and other aspirations, especially for your primary relationships and financial growth. Unplanned entanglements often satisfy temporary demands without any consideration of your life's potential and personal worth unless you learn how to properly exchange and market yourself as a specific kind of social currency, which also requires a great deal of thinking and spiritual guidance. But even in this, in some cases, you must be willing to narrow your field of focus in order to succeed.

The former captain of the Los Angeles Lakers, Magic Johnson—in an interview posted on YouTube with young Maverick Carter, who is widely known as LeBron James's agent—pointed out that both of their business endeavor was to *change* athletes' mindset to *believe* that they can excel on the court and on the field but that they can also be successful as CEOs and in the business rooms.

> A lot of times, what happens is as athletes or minorities, we hurt ourselves because we *think* we can't achieve that! It's not for us, or we don't want to go through what it takes to get there. But I was the dude that said, "Oh show me, show me the way. Give me the road map."

Today, Magic is known widely as the renowned former basketball player with unquestionable championship grace on the courts who had to reinvent himself after discovering he'd contracted the HIV virus. A friend of Jerry Buss—the deceased billionaire owner of the Los Angeles Lakers, who took him under his tutelage and made him the richest professional basketball player in the NBA—Magic had always aspired to succeed as a CEO, executive, or businessman. After his HIV discovery, Magic relentlessly pursued Michael Ortiz as his agent and mentor in order to fulfill his dreams of becoming a successful businessman.

Now a Bloomberg Game Changer with an estimated net worth of $650 million and with MJE worth a reported $1 billion, Johnson is one of the most successful Black businessmen in the US simply because he was willing to take the risk beyond his comprehension but within his ability to dream.

Magic Johnson Enterprises serves as a catalyst for fostering community and economic empowerment by providing access to high-quality entertainment, products, and services that answer to the demands of multicultural communities.

I am always amazed by the fact that Christianity expects the world to be influenced by its noninvolvement or noninclusion in the things that impact our social existence most, especially while we struggle daily with being different morally. Although Jesus said, "You are the *salt* of the earth; and the *light* of the world. A *city* that is set on a hill cannot be hidden," the world has mastered replenishing and subduing the earth, while the church has focused primarily on being fruitful and multiplying. This is important because the majority of the things we as kingdom citizens desire to do for our families requires us to go to the world's venues—employment; education; amusement; recreation; health; entertainment to include media, music, and movies; etc.

Before I conclude this chapter I thought it would be both challenging to some and encouraging to many others to highlight a very successful individual, who constantly uses his convictions to think and function out of the box. Mainly because he selflessly uses his success to not only inspire, provoke and motivate others. But humbly provide support systems, successful others, and a variety of platforms that he has access to in multiple ways, to assist others in succeeding in their endeavors.

**Honorable I introduce the Great Helper,**
**Shaquille O'Neal, the king of franchises: who has opened 155 burger joints, 40 gyms and earned a $400 million fortune.**

The former NBA player has a Ph.D. in education and a master's degree in business. He has owned over a hundred Five Guys restaurants, 150 car washes and a movie theater, and he now runs his own fast food chain. Those attending the International Franchise Association conference in San Diego were surprised to discover that the gathering's speakers included former NBA player Shaquille O'Neal.

O'Neal told CNBC during the event "I learned from the great Magic Johnson that it's okay to be a basketball star, but at some point you want to start investing in businesses."

Gone is the 21-year-old athlete who spent his first million in a single day, after signing with the Orlando Magic in 1992. Thanks to his 19 seasons as a professional athlete and his investments in different restaurant franchises and fast-food chains, among other businesses, O'Neal now has a net worth of $400 million (just under €380 million). He is one of the five richest players in the NBA, only

# GREAT THINKING

preceded by Michael Jordan, Magic Johnson, Junior Bridgeman and Lebron James, who a net worth of $1 billion.

Thinking out of the box as an example to many O'Neal says **"The franchise is a simple model. If it works, you follow the rules and it will continue to work. If you stick to the values you've learned, you can't go wrong."** This philosophy has made O'Neal, who has an MBA from the University of Phoenix and a Ph.D. in Education, into the king of franchising. "It's just something to have on my resume for when I go back to reality. Someday I might have to put down a basketball and have a regular 9-5 like everyone else," the player said at his graduation ceremony a decade ago.

Since he announced his retirement in 2011, the NBA star has become the owner of 155 Five Guys hamburger establishments, which represented 10% of the total company. (He would later sell the franchises.) O'Neal also owns 17 Auntie Anne's Pretzels restaurants and has invested in nine Papa John's restaurants.

In addition to putting his money into 150 car washes, 40 24-hour gyms and a movie theater in his native Newark, he also runs his own fast-food chain. In 2018, he founded the Big Chicken brand of chicken sandwiches. With more than 10 establishments in the city of Las Vegas, the businessman was looking to expand to other American cities such as Austin and Phoenix. The franchise's chicken sandwiches also now appear on the menus of the Carnival cruise company, of which he calls himself the "Chief Fun Officer." His passion for food has even led to a recipe book that he published. With a cover featuring burgers, brownies and fried chicken, Shaq's Family Style promises "championship recipes for feeding family and friends." He says in the text that he wanted to call the book "recipes for dummies" and that he opted for simple recipes from his childhood: **Things I love to eat, places I've been, people I love, things I believe in and some of my best inventions**," he writes, referring to the Big Chicken recipes.

Believe in the business and follow your instincts.

As he has stated in interviews, the four-time NBA championship winner has always known that money could disappear just as quickly as it appeared. According to a Study published in sports illustrated, 60% of former NBA players go bankrupt within five years of retiring.

When O'Neal retired from the NBA, he had earned more than $292 million (€277 million) from basketball, in addition to another $220 million (€209 million) in sponsorships and advertisements for brands such as Oreos, Pepsi and Reebok. But before he said goodbye to the courts, O'Neal had already started thinking out of the box when he made his big investment: buying Google stock. "One day, I hear these two gentlemen talking about Google search engines […] I would like to invest in this. My guy hooked it up, we invested and then I forgot all about it," he explained in 2019 in an interview with the Wall Street Journal. In the same interview, **he confessed that his success as an entrepreneur is based on never investing in or advertising for a company whose products he would not use himself.** "My skill is, if something comes across my desk, and I don't believe in it, I won't even look at it," O'Neal explained.

He also recalled that the Wheaties cereal company wanted to make him the face of the brand, but he refused because he preferred their rivals: Frosted Flakes—he would later appear on their cereal boxes. He admitted, though, that following his instincts has not always worked for him. O'Neal, who is also a DJ, actor and talk show host, recalled how one of his biggest regrets was not doing business with the CEO of Starbucks. "my agent calls me up and he says 'Howard Schultz wants to do business with you, And I'm like coffee? Because growing up, in my household, I'd never seen a Black person drink coffee," he told American journalist Graham Bensinger. "So, I took the great Howard Schutz in his face," he continued, "and said, 'Black people don't drink coffee, sir. I don't think it's going to work. And you should have seen his face."

Although following his beliefs did not always yield the most favorable results for him. O'Neal never stop pursuing his passion as an entrepreneur and for bringing assistance to others who were struggling to raise the bar of their own personal business. In my book,

# GREAT THINKING

this man Shaq, who learned from the great magic Johnson to start investing in businesses is a prime example of what our society needs more of, **GREAT THINKERS** who empowers others to *think* and *achieve* the ultimate.

# Be Willing to Pay the Price

*Too many people want to have mountaintop experiences at rock-bottom prices and that just doesn't work. Greatness doesn't come at a discount. If you want true greatness, you have to pay the full price for it.*
—Damilola Oluwatoyinbo

A great percentage of the cost one can willingly pay is intentional reading to enhance their ability to visualize, grasp, and imagine.

I once read a quote that said, "If you think education is expensive, try ignorance."

Another quote that I heard as a young aspiring teenager that both insulted and inspired me was "if you want to hide something from a Black, put it in a book!"

Recently, I read a column reposted by Rachel Lakhi—a self-employed educator who lives in Johannesburg, South Africa—titled, "Blacks Don't Read."

This is very deep and, unfortunately, very true! This is a heavy piece, and a Caucasian wrote it, Lakhi said. The piece is titled "They Are Still Our Slaves."

We can continue to reap profits from the Blacks without the effort of physical slavery. Look at the current methods of containment that they use on themselves: *ignorance, greed,* and *selfishness.*

Their *ignorance* is the primary weapon of containment. A great man once said, "The best way to hide something from Black people is to put it in a book." We live now in the information age. They have gained the opportunity to read any book on any subject through the efforts of their fight for freedom, yet they refuse to read.

## GREAT THINKING

There are numerous books readily available at Borders, Barnes & Noble, and Amazon.com, not to mention their own Black bookstores that provide solid blueprints to reach economic equality (which should have been their fight all along), but few read consistently, if at all.

The prophet Hosea identified ignorance as the grounds of God's controversy with Israel in 758 BC. Notice:

> My people are destroyed for lack of knowledge [of My law, where I reveal My will]. Because you [the priestly nation] have rejected knowledge, I will also reject you from being My priest.

Ignorance is a lack of knowledge. The word *ignorant* is an adjective that describes a person in the state of being unaware and can describe individuals who deliberately ignore or disregard important information or facts or individuals who are also unaware of important information or facts.

Ignorance can appear in three different types: factual ignorance (absence of knowledge of some fact), objectual ignorance (unacquaintance with some object), and technical ignorance (absence of knowledge of how to do something).

This makes *reading* a tremendous asset to thinking, and according to PBS, reading is essential for a child's success.

All too often, the barriers faced by children with difficulty reading outweigh their desire to read, and without proper guidance, they never overcome them.

Learning to read is a sequential process; each new skill builds on the mastery of previously learned skills. Early on, for example, children learn to break down words into their most basic sounds in a process called decoding. Later, they begin to comprehend the meaning of words; sentences; and, ultimately, entire passages of text.

Decoding creates the foundation on which all other reading skills are built. For many, decoding comes naturally, quickly becoming an automatic process. For people who struggle to decode words, however, the process requires such extreme concentration that they often miss much of the meaning in what they read. Indeed, according to many experts, decoding problems are at the root of most reading disabilities.

The following medical and educational facts emphasize the importance of recognizing and addressing a reading problem early on, when a child still has the opportunity to maximize the development of fundamental skills like decoding and further underscore the importance of early intervention:

* Roughly 85 percent of children diagnosed with learning difficulties have a primary problem with reading and related language skills. Most reading disabilities are neurodevelopmental in nature.
* Neurodevelopmental problems don't go away, but they can be managed.
* Most children with reading disabilities can become proficient readers and can learn strategies for success in school.
* When a child's reading disability is identified early, that child is more likely to learn strategies that will raise his or her reading to grade level.

Of all the skills children learn, reading is arguably the most important. It is a means of gaining knowledge about many different subjects and of understanding the world.

Today, especially in the developed world, it is considered a fundamental skill required for success. Unfortunately, for many children with reading disabilities, learning to read is one of the most arduous and frustrating activities they will ever face. All too often, the barriers they face outweigh their desire to read, and without proper guidance, they never overcome them.

I think it's a small price to pay in order to ensure that you are being guided by appropriate knowledge. But you must be willing to get rid of the excuses and take responsibility for yourself.

Wise man King Solomon wrote,

> The slothful man saith, There is a lion without, I shall be slain in the streets. (Proverbs 22:13)

I often share this quote because here, the king shares an insightful observation regarding individuals who use their thinking powers to defend neglect, procrastination, and laziness over duty, productivity, labor, and good business.

He illustrates how many people are ruined by their slothfulness, and yet still they offer excuses for themselves, ingeniously cheating on themselves. Their pretenses are all vain and frivolous. So feather-brained and empty-headed, they dream up the lion that emphasizes how they frighten themselves from real duties and responsibilities by imaginary difficulties. The individual puts on this act to avoid those that solicit them for labor and duty that they might assume responsibility for their own affairs.

An *indolent* person is someone who has or shows a disposition to avoid exertion (mental or physical effort) commonly referred to as lazy and slothful because they won't do what they should do in order to succeed. Or they won't do what they can to avoid becoming a problem or obstacle for others.

Jesus referred to indolence as *idleness* because this individual's negligence, idle, and noncompliant thoughts usually generate inactive, useless, ineffective, and nonoperative words and actions.

It's important to understand that God's system designed to improve life through kingdom-principles is often lost in the mental and physical indolence or neglected efforts of His people and their faithless practices.

Herein to be *idle* is to be lazy, indolent, slothful, remiss, inactive, negligent, and uninspired.

Three of the common allies of stagnation from idleness are procrastination, complacency, and excuses. I frequently use this metaphor to make the point. Idle is the car sitting in the garage waiting for the *key of interest* to crank it in order to fulfill its *purpose*.

Although the *mind* is the state and place of thousands of traveling thoughts in the form of ideas, dreams, visions, plans, logics, and reasonings, if the *key of interest* doesn't crank it, it may never be initiated to fulfill its *purpose*.

# FINACE BUSH

The lyrics to this song by Iggy Pop clarify the point.

> I'm bored
> I'm the chairman of the bored
> I'm a lengthy monologue
> I'm livin' like a dog
> I'm bored
> I bore myself to sleep at night
> I bore myself in broad daylight
> 'Cause I'm bored
> Just another slimy bore
> I'm free to bore my well-bought friends
> And spend my cash until the end
> 'Cause I'm bored

The problem is whenever you fail to use your mind purposefully, the adversary uses it adversely but creatively. Like cancer, he uses your mind malignantly, causing it to become a fertile spring for evil.

Here again, our minds are meant to dwell on things intentionally. Since emptying one's mind is an impossibility and is downright dangerous, our minds constantly need and crave focus.

We can choose to focus on important things, righteous things, and things that benefit us and others, but by the same token, our minds involuntarily have the potential to dwell on negative things, fantasies, and unimportant things, which is the juncture at which our minds can lead us astray.

As for the devil, he wants us to dwell on negative things, and though he cannot *make us* focus on what is negative, his *modus operandi* is to exert on us a malignant influence, an influence similar to how he *imposed* his logic on Adam and Eve in the Garden many years ago.

When we let down our guard, our minds can be led astray by negative things such as lust, pride, envy, revenge, resentment, jealousy, hatred, unforgiveness, depression, and rage, to name a few.

# GREAT THINKING

It is important for every person to strive to become their maximum self. Your calling is not something that others can discover for you. It's what you constantly feel inside of yourself—an inner craving, stimulation, or motivation that surfaces sometimes when you least expect it. It sparks your interest, but you fail to commit it to your imagination.

It is the thing that gives you energy because it's actually *the thing* that you are supposed to do. And nobody can tell you what that really is but God. You know it inside yourself.

It is for this reason that Christ in us is the state, standard, and the true starting point of discovering our personal identity, purpose, and personality.

Before concluding this chapter, I want to introduce the word *bored*, which is the opposite of the words *interest* and *entertainment*. *Bored* is a state of mind that has become a present-tense reality for multitudes of potentially great minds.

I think it's necessary because *bored* happens when you're feeling weary and unoccupied or you lack interest in your current activity.

Have you noticed that kids will hang around all day bored stiff when they aren't taught or trained to explore, examine, and explain?

*A grandma recently stated*, "I noticed that when my granddaughter gets bored, she just stares out the window all day."

In many cases, constant boredom is an indication of low self-esteem or a lack of self-esteem.

Psychologists say that *self-esteem* reflects a person's overall subjective *emotional evaluation of his or her own worth*. It is your personal judgment of yourself as well as your attitude toward the *self*.

*Self-esteem is important* to an individual because the person who has low self-esteem or no self-esteem may never see themselves as important enough to matter, be included, or be considered, which can make individuals candidates for depression.

Here's an important discovery I made as I refused to accept boredom and began to find ways to multiply my personal value in my own eyes while paying the price to overcome mediocrity.

Suddenly, an unanticipated observation became a constant and exciting reality for me. I realized in areas that I would visit and associate frequently that my new inner self-assessment was being adopted and embraced by the outside world, which encouraged and motivated me immensely. To be seen in a more favorable context by your peers and colleagues is a tremendous boost to an individual's self-esteem.

I once heard someone say, "The only valid price tag is the one we attach to ourselves. If we price ourselves too low, the world will agree. But if we price ourselves with the very best, the world will willingly accept that valuation."

Lack of initiative many times results in an attitude breakdown, which causes blame toward other significant and unimportant persons in our lives for not making sure we were esteemed, much like the ten spies in Numbers 13:33–14:4, who refused to be influenced by Moses and Caleb because of the many whispers and speculations.

Notice that they said, "There we saw the giants (the descendants of Anak came from the giants), and we were like grasshoppers in our own sight, and so we were in their sight."

Point is, the less certain we are about our own *identity*, the more likely we are to compare ourselves with others inappropriately. You are fearfully and wonderfully made, so you have a unique purpose. Be yourself!

Notice how these unfavorable comparisons caused these individuals to function beneath their grace and potential and forfeit God's goodness toward them. This happened simply because they neglected to see themselves as God (Creator and Father) said they were.

> The more you praise and celebrate your life,
> the more there is in life to celebrate.
> —Oprah Winfrey

# Improving Your Brain Function

Since the emergence of the twentieth century, man's achievements in science and technology have astonished the world. From cures for deadly diseases to discoveries of other galaxies, man has reached beyond the horizon of his greatest imaginations to bring us from radio and television to the internet.

Those who pioneered the way made tremendous personal and relational sacrifices in order to achieve their goals for the advancement of society. Their willingness to assume responsibility for modernization and the advancement of human or civil rights has resulted in freedom to use their time purposefully and constructively to arrange convenient lifestyles to complement their desires and, for many successful accomplishers, an extravagant family inheritance. They reflect the value and benefit of thinking one's way to freedom.

A quote from Sigmund Freud merged with Edison's quote helps me further establish the point I want to emphasize for this essential *exchange* in *thinking*.

The quote is

> Most people do not really want freedom, because *freedom involves responsibility*, and most people are frightened of responsibility.

When I first heard this quote, it literally stopped me in my tracks because honestly, I tried, as a Black man, to get offended with Freud's use of the words "freedom and responsibility" to make his point. Although I'd been seeking answers for why so many adults seem to live irresponsibly, especially after marriage and with children, the truth of the matter is that this quote actually gets to the heart of the issue in ways that cannot be denied.

In order to observe how Freud's quote may serve as a description of the society we're now a part of, I decided to do a random experiment on a group of Bible students by assigning two duties to see how swiftly they responded. The first duty was a hands-on job task already prepared for initiation but would require much more physical effort than thinking.

The second duty was a simple thought-based assignment that would require little physical effort.

I returned after ninety minutes only to discover that the first group had gladly completed their task, while the second group was actually apprehensive about getting started because they didn't want to have to *think*. They wanted the freedom to do so without the demands of thinking like the first group.

Although I was disappointed, this experiment helped me to understand why many people may never escape the day-to-day frustrations of depending upon others to do their most critical thinking.

Since this experiment, I've noticed that a lot of people prefer complaining about life's challenges and the difficulties they encounter from day to day rather than analytically and constructively thinking ahead to gain mastery over their struggles.

Einstein once said, "Imagination is more important than knowledge."

Great thinkers understand this statement because they too are aware of the fact that in many ways, *imagination rules the world*!

In fact, to support this, Einstein also said, "No problem can be solved from the same level of consciousness that created it."

In this, he is saying that sometimes you, as an individual, have to learn how to trust your higher level of consciousness, internal instincts, or what I identify as your internal unction from God to keep working on the solution while you rest away from the problem.

Sometimes I literally have to put difficult things aside and walk away to avoid complicating them so I can rest apart from it in order to use my available time on other things I can easily resolve. Later I'd return to what seemed difficult, and the answer or solution would leap at me. Or while working on something else, a stunning revelation would unveil itself to me, leaving me in awe.

## *A good example*

Recently, I was in the process of refurbishing some kitchen cabinets while customizing them to complement a new pair of refrigerator units. Initially, I knew it would be a simple task. But after my wife decided to add other appliances within the same space, I lost concept and would have become frustrated if I wasn't accustomed to pulling away until I could visualize it complete. One day while finishing the woodwork in an adjoining room, I passed by the area to pick up some more material. Suddenly I glimpsed the area and saw it in the eye of my mind as complete. Immediately I conceived how to proceed with the project and it became an easy task.

Trusting the Spirit of God to keep working with your higher consciousness on solutions to your challenges will provide tremendous growth in your relationship with God and your personal unction to function. You might be surprised, like I was, at how simple a complex problem can become when we give ourselves the time and space to be mindfully acquainted with it through meditation.

However, *this means you have to keep thinking.*

Wise man Solomon said, "Without a vision or redeeming revelation from God people perish or cast of restraints."

Habakkuk, the prophet, said, "Write the vision and make it plain enough to be read at a glance."

God encouraged Joshua by saying, "This book of the laws and principles that govern life shall not depart from your mouth but you shall meditate day and night so that you may be careful to do everything written in it. Then you will make your way prosperous and you shall have good success."

Thomas Edison said, "The first requisite for success is the ability to apply your physical and mental energies to one problem incessantly without growing weary."

He also said, "If we did all the things we are capable of, we would literally astound ourselves."

I recently read an article written by Lana Burgess titled "What Percentage of Our *Brain* Do We Use?" In this article, her team explored how much of the brain a person uses. They also challenged some widely held myths and revealed some interesting facts about the brain.

A person's brain determines how they experience the world around them. The brain weighs about three pounds and contains around 100 billion neurons—cells that carry information.

The report stated, "According to a survey from 2013, around 65 percent of Americans believe that we only use 10 percent of our brain."

But this is just a myth, according to an interview with neurologist Barry Gordon in *Scientific American*. He explained that the majority of the brain is almost always active.

The 10 percent myth was also debunked in a study published in *Frontiers in Human Neuroscience*.

One common brain-imaging technique called functional magnetic resonance imaging (fMRI) can measure activity in the brain while a person is performing different tasks.

Using this and similar methods, researchers show that most of our brain is in use most of the time, even when a person is performing a very simple action.

A lot of the brain is even active when a person is resting or sleeping.

The percentage of the brain in use at any given time varies from person to person. It also depends on what a person is doing or thinking about.

Where does the 10 percent myth come from?

It's not clear how this myth began, but there are several possible sources.

In an article published in a 1907 edition of the journal *Science*, psychologist and author William James argued that humans only use part of their mental resources. However, he did not specify a percentage.

The figure was referenced in Dale Carnegie's 1936 book *How to Win Friends and Influence People*. The myth was described as something the author's college professor used to say.

There is also a belief among scientists that neurons (nerve cells) make up around 10 percent of the brain's cells. This may have contributed to the 10 percent myth.

The myth has been repeated in articles, TV programs, and films, which helps to explain why it is so widely believed.

The article also stated that like any other organ, the brain is affected by a person's lifestyle, diet, and the amount that they exercise.

To improve the health and function of the brain, a person can do the following things.

1. Eat a balanced diet—eating well improves overall health and well-being. It also reduces the risk of developing health issues that may lead to dementia, including
   * cardiovascular disease,
   * midlife obesity,
   * type 2 diabetes.

   The following foods promote brain health:
   * Fruits and vegetables with dark skins. Some are rich in vitamin E, such as spinach, broccoli, and blueberries. Others are rich in beta carotene, including red peppers and sweet potatoes. Vitamin E and beta carotene promote brain health.
   * Oily fish. These types of fish, such as salmon, mackerel, and tuna, are rich in omega-3 fatty acids, which may support cognitive function.
   * Walnuts and pecans. They are rich in antioxidants, which promote brain health.
   * There is a selection of walnuts and pecans available for purchase online.

2. Exercise regularly—regular exercise also reduces the risk of health problems that may lead to dementia. Cardiovascular

activities, such as walking briskly for thirty minutes a day, can be enough to reduce the risk of brain function declining. Other accessible and inexpensive options include
* bike riding,
* jogging,
* swimming.

3. Keep the brain active—the more a person uses their brain, the better their mental functions become. For this reason, brain-training exercises are a good way to maintain overall brain health. A recent study conducted over ten years found that people who used brain-training exercises reduced the risk of dementia by 29 percent. The most effective training focused on increasing the brain's speed and ability to process complex information quickly.

*Here again,* the quote from Sigmund Freud that disturbs me most is "most people do not really want freedom, because *freedom involves responsibility,* and most people are frightened of responsibility."

Notice the three words I emphasized in Freud's quote: "freedom involves responsibility."

It's a frightening thing to consider the possibility of losing many generations to come because of their inability to maintain freedom due to their *fright* of *responsibility*. God has never given man responsibility without the *ability* to perform it. But one must be committed to *thinking*! Or they may spend their entire lives at the mercy of someone who does.

There is no reason to fear *responsibility*. Its purpose is to generate great *thinkers* who will use their opportunities to manifest their creative genius like God.

In order to help you remain mentally conscious of your need to keep God and His Word at the center of your thinking exchanges, remember Isaiah 26:3: "I will keep him in perfect peace, whose *mind* is stayed on *me*."

The word *peace* in Hebrew, *Shalom,* means "nothing missing, nothing broken." Everything God has promised, He will perform.

It's important to make this statement because in spite of the multitude of disappointments and letdowns you may have experienced personally from failed attempts or with men, you can still trust God. So get yourself in position to *try* again.

Sometimes the reason trusting God is neglected or never even considered is because we systematically fail to keep God distinguished in our thinking apart from our daily experiences with men.

# Overcoming Oppositions and Hurdles to Thinking

A great example of how the illusion of risk can generate hurdles that are difficult to overcome through thinking is found in the example of Israel under the leadership of Moses. Today, these people are viewed as the ultimate reference for the effects of a negative *self-image* or low self-esteem. Israel's failure to enter the promised land on schedule also serves as an example of how bad influences over non-thinkers adversely affect right courses and cancel the reception of many blessings.

How does over two million people live in a land of bondage over four hundred years, waiting for a promise to fulfill? And at the appointed time, they

* experience ten miraculous plagues to obtain their deliverance;
* get delivered and totally set free from the bondage of oppression and oppressors;
* cross a parted Red *Sea*—not a river, stream, pond, or, lake, but a *sea*!—on dry land;
* then journeyed only eleven days to get to the place promised that they've desired all that time. I'm saying they literally got where they could see *it* and sent twelve spies in to *it* for forty days to confirm that the land was just like God said *it* was;
* took a cluster of fruit from *it* but still not go in and possess *it*.

# GREAT THINKING

Or better yet, how does over two million people allow themselves to become afraid of entering into a land they can clearly see that God prepared for them but allow ten of twelve spies to come back more afraid to enter than two spies that saw the *same* thing?

I have witnessed how *illusions*, over time, create *suspicions* in the minds of those who fail to condition their thinking. And these unruled thoughts generate *suppositions*, which oppose faith.

Satan's trick is to influence you to *think* according to your limited perception of the *appearance* of things to you. He knows that "how you *see* you is how you *be* you."

Eventually, these sense triggers will generate insecurities that will result in a fearful or doubtful understanding.

## *Remember, the devil is a liar!*

A "lie" is a nonexistent existence! Although it exists, it has absolutely *no* affirmable proof. A lie carries the seed in the mind of a potential harvest you can experience in your life through imagination. You must learn to "cast illegal thoughts down and bring them under obedience to Christ."

This is important because the *mind cannot distinguish* the difference between an experience in *real* life from an experience *you create* in your own *mind*.

By creating and visualizing different things you would like to happen in your life or by allowing your mind to repeatedly ponder a *lie* from the devil, you are actually making them happen *internally*.

On the other side, this is why many law-of-attraction teachers talk about vision boards and creative visualization. By intentionally *training* your *mind* to *see* and *feel* what you want, you are actually *attracting* it.

In addition to the visual exercise, there are also other parts you need to consider when getting the law of attraction to work.

Notice Jesus's reply to inappropriate thinking:

> You are of your father the devil, and it is your will to practice the desires [which are char-

> acteristic] of your father. He was a murderer from the beginning, and does not stand in the truth because there is no *truth* in him. When he lies, he speaks what is natural to him, for he is a *liar* and the *father* of *lies* and half-truths.
>
> But because I speak the truth, you do not believe Me [and continue in your unbelief]. (John 8:44–45 AMP)

In other words, if you suppose that physical pain is a sign of a sickness or a real problem, your suspicious mind can produce an internal ghost or belief that will support your theory and find ways to confirm it.

Here again, the *mind* cannot tell the difference between an experience in real life or an experience you create in it. The supposition of a ghost can affect the strength and capability of the power of God's Spirit in you in a very negative way.

A supposition is an idea or statement or satanic whisper that someone believes or assumes to be true, although they may have *no* evidence for it.

Neuropsychologist point out that hypochondria is a condition in which a person is excessively worried about having a physical illness though it's meaning has repeatedly changed due to redefinitions in its source metaphors. It has been claimed that this debilitating condition results from an inaccurate perception of the condition of body or mind despite the absence of an actual medical diagnosis.

We often perplex and frighten ourselves with phantasms, which are creatures and illusions from our own imagination. It must be understood that phantasms are strong illusions seen in the mind but have *no* physical reality. *They are satanic lies!* These "lies" are designed purposefully to deceive you.

Fear of failure is also a *ghost* designed to stop you from moving toward experiencing the enrichment power and potential ability of Christ in you, which requires confidence, courage, and strength.

For this reason, billionaire Warren Buffett said it is important for you to *prepare to succeed* because "Risk come from *not* knowing what you're doing. Risk is a part of God's game, alike for men and nations." He later said, "I always knew I was going to be rich. I don't think I ever doubted it for a minute."

The fainthearted and those who fail to *think* through their challenges hardly ever experience the dynamic power of God's grace because of the ghostly appearance of obstacles and hurdles to the natural mind and natural senses.

Let me offer a word of caution to you as you journey with me through these pages.

To the fainthearted, the coward, and the dependent, here's something you should know. Desire and opportunity is often generated to make your life better, but illusion from unchallenged logic and untested reasoning paints an internal mental picture of a fearful outcome that makes *trying* to succeed more difficult than staying in *familiar* misery.

How does an individual overcome the *illusion* of a *risk failure*?

Notice how I did not say an actual failure but the *illusion* of a risk failure, especially, when the creator Himself has guaranteed you will succeed by trusting and obeying Him.

Let's understand that *illusion* is a thing that is, or is likely to be, wrongly perceived or interpreted by the senses. It is a deceptive appearance or impression that causes tension between mirages, fantasies, and reality, which is a primary reason Jesus said, "Judge not according to the appearance, but judge righteously."

Let me suggest to you that there is an appointed alignment full of opportunities more important for your mind than the constant distractions of appearance, especially regarding how others are living and what they're saying about you.

In fact, 2 Corinthians 10:5 says we're supposed to be "casting down arguments, reasonings, and every high thing that exalts itself against the *knowledge* of God, bringing *every thought* into captivity to the obedience of Christ."

Without a definite purpose, we have no defined or definitive pursuit to keep our mental energies and thoughts regulated. Without knowledge of purpose, life becomes an endless string of activities with little or no significance. A knowledge of purpose increases the mind's ability to imagine future realities that include favorable outcomes.

An imagined reality is an event or environment in the *future* that you want to *move* toward. *Why?* It narrows down your *field* of *focus*.

Since meditation is the influence of faith and fear and constructive thinking is the influence of creative imagination, this question must be asked, what are you thinking about the majority of your *time?*

This question is vitally important because Jesus said in Matthew 12:35, "A good man out of the good treasure of his heart brings forth good things, and an evil man out of the evil treasure brings forth evil things."

A good example of this can be seen in Genesis 6:5, 7–8:

> And God saw that the wickedness of man was great in the earth, and that every imagination of the thoughts of his heart was only evil continually. So the LORD said, "I will destroy man whom I have created from the face of the earth, both man and beast, creeping thing and birds of the air, for I am sorry that I have made them." But Noah found *grace* in the eyes of the LORD.

In other words, while all others were selfishly consumed and possessed with the imagination of only evil things, Noah was prompted through Grace and convicted by the Spirit to pursue a vision from God to build a vessel never seen before. He demonstrated to us the power of thought mixed with faith. *Notice:*

> By faith Noah, being warned of God of things not seen as yet, moved with fear, prepared an ark to the saving of his house; by the which he condemned the world, and became heir of the righteousness which is by faith. (Hebrews 11:7 KJV)

All I'm saying in this is that many people cannot be depended upon to go very far in life because they lack a vision that gives personal distinction and something significant to pursue for personal fulfillment—a vision that's well-planned, is easy to follow, and generates a constant appetite to keep the individual hungry for its manifestation.

*Like Israel's ten spies*, when you don't know *who* you are, you can *fit* in with anybody. When you don't know *where* you're headed, *anywhere* will do. When you don't know *what* your purpose is, *anything* will suffice for the moment.

Offenses and obstacles were never designed to determine the longevity of our pursuits. They are obstacles designed to instill the toughness and discipline necessary to endure for the long haul. This makes it easy to see why some people may never accomplish anything meaningful or significant.

Remember this, those who commit to *duty* before *thought* or duty without thinking will always be subjected by their non-thinking to live and coexist in another person's idea, dream, vision, concept, or environment.

Life and living without *identity* and *purpose* causes an individual like a plant to eventually wither away. Over extended periods of time, it becomes increasingly difficult to maintain peace, joy, and fulfillment without purpose.

One reason we walk by faith, not by sight, is because sight paints the illusion that things are against us when in essence, they may really be for us. Sometimes it even seems as if people who love us do not have our best interest at heart. But it only appears that way because of a lack of information or our failure to solicit correct understanding.

To further establish the need for great thinkers in this significant time of our existence, I thought it would be good to revisit several renowned patriots in order to reflect upon their views about intense constructive thinking, along with its impact upon social progressivism and the labor movement. To begin, I decided to first list the patriot's quote, then discuss each of the quote's meaning as food for thought.

## Patriarchal sayings

> He who starts behind in the great race of life must forever remain behind or run faster than the man in front. (Benjamin E. Mays)

Notice the emphasis Dr. Mays places on knowing how and where your beginning begins. Those who start behind do not have the leisure of time to procrastinate and remain idle as those who start with an advantage. They must garner up every waking moment to extend themselves in a way to first catch up in the great race of life before getting ahead of those who started first with advantages.

Carter G. Woodson is quoted as saying,

> At this moment, then, the Negroes must begin to do the very thing which they have been told that they cannot do. They still have some money, and they have need to supply. They must begin immediately to pool their earnings and organize industries to participate in supplying social and economic demands. If the Negroes are to remain forever removed from the producing atmosphere, and the present discrimination continues, there will be nothing left for them to do.

In this, Woodson demonstrates his consciousness of the importance of the Negroes' need to first unlearn what was deceitfully planted in their belief system, then strategize to organize methods and systems that would allow them to account for supplying their own social and economic demands while also establishing a presence in the producing atmosphere, which is the reason I pointed out earlier that "duty before thought or duty without thinking always subjects the non-thinker to live and coexist in another person's idea, dream, vision, concept, or environment." This cycle, in turn, limits and restricts the individual and those families from the opportunities to succeed relative to the economy they're a part of.

I refer to this as *the great waste of mental assets* primarily because here again, a person must really decide if they truly want *freedom*, which brings me back to my reason for saying "those who fail to think and plan survive from the wind of the wings of those who do."

Today's advanced society offers a variety of opportunities for every individual to succeed.

Alongside other races and cultures, our African American culture has a plenitudinous supply of visionaries and dreamers—men, women, and children with ideas, ideals, systems, multiple types of designs and designers, organizers, planners, inventors of a variety of sorts and subjects. There are also too many multi-gifted, skilled, and talented individuals in our race for us to neglect learning how to advance in ways that will support and supply our own economy in this opportunistic society.

Besides all this, there is an indigenous or autochthonous side to God and godliness that is missing from the daily practices and understanding of the religious right that promotes an ungodly fear against righteous gain.

In right scriptural context, righteous gain is simply God's *righteous* way of prospering, increasing and multiplying kingdom citizens through and by *faith*.

For this reason again, I quote Sigmund Freud, who said, "Most people do not really want freedom, because *freedom involves responsibility*, and most people are frightened of *responsibility*."

Clearly an individual, family, or cultural community must first decide if they truly want freedom and the responsibility that will accompany it. That decision should be accompanied by a commitment to do whatever it takes to obtain a goal and the freedom desired.

Next, I think it's important to explore *the means for advancement in this society*.

To begin, remember that Thomas Edison said, "The first requisite for success is the ability to apply your physical and mental energies to one problem incessantly without growing weary."

Edison also said, "If we did all the things we are capable of, we would literally astound ourselves."

In order to further explain advancement means and measures to coincide with Carter G. Woodson's instructional quote, I found an insightful compilation of information in *Wikipedia* titled "Means of Production," which may help me to also explain why some cultures have more perplexed social systems than others. To enhance everyone's ability to use this significant information, I've also written a comprehensive dictionary at the end of the chapter titled "Relative Terms" explaining each of the highlighted relevant words, terms, and phrases.

# Means of Production

To begin, in economics and sociology, the means of production (also called capital goods) are physical and nonfinancial inputs used in the production of economic value. These include raw materials, facilities, machinery, and tools used in the production of goods and services.

In the terminology of classical economics, the means of production are regarded as the "factors of production" minus financial and human capital.

The social means of production are capital goods and assets that require organized collective labor effort, as opposed to individual effort, to operate on. The ownership and organization of the social means of production is a *key factor* in categorizing and defining different types of economic systems.

The means of production includes two broad categories of objects: instruments of labor (tools, factories, infrastructure, etc.) and subjects of labor (natural resources and raw materials). People operate on the subjects of labor using the instruments of labor to create a product, or stated another way, labor acting on the means of production creates a good. To fully grasp this concept, it's important to explore different societies and how they function.

## *Different societies and how they function*

For example, in an agrarian society, the principal means of production is the soil and the shovel. In an industrial society, the means of production become social means of production and include factories and mines. In a knowledge economy, computers and networks are means of production. In a broad sense, the "means of production"

## *Marxian analysis*

The analysis of the technological sophistication of the means of production and how they are *owned* is a central component in the Marxist theoretical framework of historical materialism and in Marxian economics.

In Marx's work and subsequent developments in Marxist theory, the process of socioeconomic evolution is based on the premise of technological improvements in the means of production. As the level of technology improves with respect to productive capabilities, existing forms of social relations become superfluous and unnecessary, creating contradictions between the level of technology in the means of production on one hand and the organization of society and its economy on the other. It's important to note that these contradictions manifest themselves in the form of class conflicts, which develop to a point where the existing mode of production becomes unsustainable, either collapsing or being overthrown in a social revolution. The contradictions are resolved by the emergence of a new mode of production based on a different set of social relations including, most notably, different patterns of ownership for the means of production.

Ownership of the means of production and control over the surplus product generated by their operation is the fundamental factor in delineating different modes of production.

Capitalism is defined as private ownership and control over the means of production, where the surplus product becomes a source of unearned income for its owners. By contrast, socialism is defined as social ownership of the means of production so that the surplus product accrues to society at large.

## *Determinant of class*

Marx's theory of class defines classes in their relation to their ownership and control of the means of production. In a capitalist society, the bourgeoisie, or the capitalist class, is the *class* that *owns* the means of production and obtain a passive income from their operation. In contrast, the proletariat, or *working class*, comprises the majority of the population that lacks access to the means of production and is therefore induced to sell their *labor power* for a wage or salary to gain access to necessities, goods, and services.

To the question of why classes exist in human societies in the first place, Karl Marx offered a historical and scientific explanation that it was the *cultural* practice of ownership of the means of production that gave rise to them.

This explanation differs dramatically from other explanations based on "differences in ability" between individuals or on religious or political affiliations giving rise to castes. These castes or classes determined if someone could marry outside of their social level, status, or echelon. This explanation is consistent with the bulk of the Marxist theory in which politics and religion are seen as mere outgrowths because they are superstructures of the basic underlying economic reality of a people.

## *Relative terms*

Factors of production are defined by German economist Karl Marx in his book *Das Kapital* as labor, subjects of labor, and instruments of labor: the term is equivalent to means of production plus labor. The factors of production are often listed in economic writings derived from the classical school as "land, labor, and capital." Marx sometimes used the term *productive forces* equivalently with *factors of production*. In *Capital*, he uses "factors of production" in his famous preface to the *Critique of Political Economy*, he uses "productive forces" (that may depend on the translation).

Production relations (German: *produktionsverhältnis*) are the relations humans enter into with one other in using the means of production to produce. Examples of such relations are employer-employee, buyer-seller, the technical division of labor in a factory, and property relations.

Mode of production (German: *produktionsweise*) means the dominant way in which production is organized in society. For instance, *capitalism* is the name for the capitalist mode of production in which the means of production are owned privately by a small class (the bourgeoisie) who profits off the labor of the working class (the proletariat). Communism is a mode of production in which the means of production are not owned by anyone but shared in common, without class-based exploitation.

An investigative review of this significant information supports my determination to bring clarity to the subject of *why* some races and cultures are subjected to *continued hardships* and *struggles*.

As you continue to journey with me, I am sure that you will be empowered to *think* and take ownership and responsibility for your existence on planet Earth.

A prominent quote from another most-admired patriarchal leader, Frederick Douglass, goes,

> Our destiny is largely in our own hands. If we find, we shall have to seek. If we succeed in the race of life it must be by our own energies, and our own exertions. Others may clear the road, but we must go forward, or be left behind in the race of life. If we remain poor and dependent, the riches of other men will not avail us. If we are ignorant, the intelligence of other men will do but a little for us. If we are foolish, The wisdom of other men will not guide us. If we are wasteful of time and money, the economy of other men will only make our destitution the more disgraceful and hurtful.

One well-known patriot whom I often describe as a "living peanut factory" took advantage of this concept of thinking before doing

# GREAT THINKING

or thought before duty. He is the most-celebrated George Washington Carver, honored today as the prominent African American scientist whose inventions included the discovery of over three hundred different uses for peanuts—such as making cooking oil, axle grease, and printer's ink.

Carver said he believed that "ninety-nine percent of the failures come from people who have the habit of making excuses."

Alexander Graham Bell, the scientist and innovator who is credited with patenting the first practical telephone, is quoted as saying, "A man, as a general rule, owes very little to what he is born with—a man is what he makes of himself. Before anything else, *preparation* is the *key* to *success*."

A modern-day contemporary, acclaimed actor Sylvester Stallone—with a baby on the way and only a little money to pay the rent on his Hollywood apartment—sat down and wrote the screenplay for *Rocky* in less than four days. Producers loved it and offered him big bucks to bring the story to life—but Stallone refused to take any offer that didn't allow him to play the lead role in the film.

His stubborn attitude landed him a far smaller paycheck than what he could have earned for his screenplay, but the risk was well worth the reward. Rocky ultimately ended up pulling in millions of dollars and skyrocketing Stallone into fame.

Another contemporary, *Vera Wang*, made a big scary career switch that became extremely rewarding. When, as a young competitive figure skater, she didn't make the 1968 US Olympic team, she pursued a career in magazine editing.

Then when she didn't get the spot for *Vogue* editor in chief, she went on to work as the design director for accessories at Ralph Lauren.

Her newfound career in fashion (coupled with a dissatisfaction with the less-than-stylish dresses available when she was planning her own wedding) led to her ultimate pursuit of a career in bridal fashion design. And today? She's one of the biggest names in the business.

Lastly, after two years at Harvard, a young Bill Gates took a *risk* that would end up giving way to the rest of his illustriously successful career.

Note, he dropped out of college to found Microsoft. Today, Harvard's most successful dropout makes a point of urging students to stay in school ("getting a degree is a much surer path to success," he's said). But the idea behind his decision to drop out is still the same—*sometimes*, a great *risk* reaps great reward!

You need to stop denying yourself the joy of living a fulfilling life and pursue a life of peace and wholesomeness.

It is clear from the words of these patriarchs that to thrive in life, one must be willing to think and act.

But what is it about life and all its demands that allows or persuades an individual to believe it's okay to live depending upon others rather than assuming responsibility for oneself?

The late Dr. Myles Munroe said,

> The greatest tragedy in life is not death, but life without a reason. It is dangerous to be alive and not know why you were given life. One of the most frustrating experiences is to have *time* but not know *why*.

Munroe also said,

> I am convinced that our Creator never intended for us to be normal—that is, to get lost in the crowd of "the norm." This is evidenced by the fact that among the 5.8 billion people on this planet, no two individuals are alike; their fingerprints, genetic code, and chromosome combinations are all distinct and unique.
>
> In reality, God created all people to be originals, but we continue to become copies of others. Too often we are so preoccupied with trying to fit in, that we never stand out. You were designed to be distinctive, special, irreplaceable, and unique, so refuse to be "normal"! Go beyond average! Do not strive to be accepted, rather strive to be your-

self. Shun the minimum; pursue the maximum. Utilize all your functions/maximize yourself!

He concluded by saying, "Use yourself up for the glory of your Creator. I admonish you: Die empty. Die fulfilled by dying unfilled."

Wise man Solomon said in Proverbs 29:18, "Where there is no revelation, the people cast off restraint; But happy is he who keeps the law."

In other words, where there is no purpose, there is no self-control, no moral conviction, and no ethical boundaries; a person may never restrain themselves to pursue anything worthwhile.

My emphasis is that until you discover your purpose in life or reason for being, life remains an *experiment* that is based on assumptions and hypothesis, which is also one of the primary reasons for so much of the corruption in the world.

The average person in America lives like they've got an eternity to discover life, not conscious that life can end any day at any time because natural life is subject to time, not eternity.

# *Listen to What Some of Our Modern-Day Visionaries Have to Say*

It is important to notice that regardless of these individuals' gender, color, race, culture, class, or backgrounds, the single common thread they possess is *vision* backed by decision, commitment, and action—their approach to it.

## *Vision quotes*

Make your vision so clear that your fears become irrelevant. (Anonymous)

If you don't have a vision you're going to be stuck in what you know. And the only thing you know is what you've already seen. (Iyanla Vanzant)

Vision without action is merely a dream. Action without vision just passes the time. Vision with action can change the world. (Joel A. Barker)

A vision is not just a picture of what could be; it is an appeal to our better selves, a call to become something more. (Rosabeth Moss Kanter)

Leadership is the capacity to translate vision into reality. (Warren G. Bennis)

## GREAT THINKING

The only thing worse than being blind is having sight but no vision. (Helen Keller)

Little girls with dreams become women with vision. (Anonymous)

You've got to think about big things while you're doing small things so that all the small things go in the right direction. (Alvin Toffler)

A dream is the creative vision for your life in the future. (Denis Waitley)

Vision is the art of seeing what is invisible to others. (Jonathan Swift)

A great leader's courage to fulfill his vision comes from passion, not position. (John Maxwell)

Hold the vision, trust the process. (Anonymous)

Don't expect people to understand your grind when God didn't give them your vision. (Anonymous)

Your vision will become clear only when you look into your heart. Who looks outside dreams. Who looks inside awakens. (Anonymous)

We are limited not by our abilities but by our vision. (Anonymous)

Where there is no vision, there is no hope. (George Washington Carver)

Chase the vision, not the money. (Tony Hsieh)

Vision is the true creative rhythm. (Robert Delaunay)

Good business leaders create a vision, articulate the vision, passionately own the vision, and relentlessly drive it to completion. (Jack Welch)

Clarify your vision. Plan with precision. (Anonymous)

Vision is a picture of the future that produces passion. (Bill Hybels)

Your thoughts shape your vision. You see what you choose to see. (Anonymous)

Vision is a destination—a fixed point to which we focus all effort. Strategy is a route—an adaptable path to get us where we want to go. (Simon Sinek)

The only limits are, as always, those of vision. (James Broughton)

One's vision is not a road map but a compass. (Peter Block)

It's important to be true to yourself and your vision. (Nicole Polizzi)

Just because a man lacks the use of his eyes doesn't mean he lacks vision. (Stevie Wonder)

# GREAT THINKING

The vision must be followed by the venture. It is not enough to stare up the steps—we must step up the stairs. (Vance Havner)

When you have a vision that is strong enough and powerful enough, nothing can stand in your way. (Lewis Howes)

A man without a vision for his future always returns to his past. (Anonymous)

Microsoft was founded with a vision of a computer on every desk, and in every home. We've never wavered from that vision. (Bill Gates)

If you want to turn a vision into reality, you have to give 100 percent and never stop believing in your dream. (Arnold Schwarzenegger)

Champions aren't made in the gyms. Champions are made from something they have deep inside them—a desire, a dream, a vision. (Muhammad Ali)

If you are working on something exciting that you really care about, you don't have to be pushed. The vision pulls you. (Steve Jobs)

Vision without execution is hallucination. (Thomas Edison)

Don't worry about being successful but work toward being significant and the success will naturally follow. (Oprah Winfrey)

You may not always have a comfortable life. And you will not always be able to solve all the world's problems all at once. But don't ever underestimate the impact you can have, because history has shown us that courage can be contagious, and hope can take on a life of its own. (Michelle Obama)

Success isn't about how your life looks to others. It's about how it feels to you. We realized that being successful isn't about being impressive, it's about being inspired. That's what it means to be true to yourself. (Michelle Obama)

Focusing your life solely on making a buck shows a certain poverty of ambition. It asks too little of yourself. Because it's only when you hitch your wagon to something larger than yourself that you realize your true potential. (Barack Obama)

It is encouraging to know that this changing world in which we live is demanding new ideas, new ways of doing things, new leaders, new inventions, new methods of teaching, new methods of marketing, new books, new literature, new features for the radio, new ideas for moving pictures.

Certainly this is an hour to possess the three major qualities common in most achievers. Although I have a hard time admitting what I'm about to say, they seem to achieve regardless of whether God is their center or not. As an aspiring individual, you need a definite purpose, the specific knowledge of what you want, and a burning desire to possess it.

*Helen Keller* became deaf, dumb, and blind shortly after birth. Despite her greatest misfortune, she has written her name indelibly in the pages of the history of the great.

# GREAT THINKING

Keller was born with her senses of sight and hearing and started speaking when she was just six months old. She started walking at the age of one.

In 1882, however, Keller contracted an illness—called "brain fever" by the family doctor—that produced a high body temperature.

The true nature of the illness remains a mystery today, though some experts believe it might have been scarlet fever or meningitis. Within a few days after the fever broke, Keller's mother noticed that her daughter didn't show any reaction when the dinner bell was rung or when a hand was waved in front of her face. Keller had lost both her sight and hearing. She was just nineteen months old.

Keller stood as a powerful example of how determination, hard work, and imagination can allow an individual to triumph over adversity. By overcoming difficult conditions with a great deal of persistence, she grew into a respected and world-renowned activist who labored for the betterment of others.

Her entire life has served as evidence that no one ever is defeated until they accept defeat as a reality.

> It's more difficult to teach ignorance to think than to teach an intelligent blind man to see the grandeur of Niagara. (Helen Keller)

*Robert Burns* was an illiterate country little boy. He was cursed by poverty and grew up to be a drunkard but, instead, turned his thoughts into poetry and thereby plucked a thorn and planted rose in its place.

*Booker T. Washington* was born in slavery, handicapped by race and color. Because he was tolerant, he had an open mind at all times on all subjects and was a dreamer. He left his imprint for good on an entire race.

*Beethoven* was deaf. *Milton* was blind, but their names will last as long as time endures because they dreamed and translated their dreams into organized thought.

*Stevie Wonder*, soul singer, released twenty-three studio albums, three soundtrack albums, four live albums, eleven compilations, one box set, and ninety-eight singles. He has had ten US number-one hits on the pop charts, as well as twenty R&B number-one hits, and has sold over 100 million records, 19.5 million of which are albums. He is one of the top-60 best-selling music artists with combined sales of singles and albums. He has thirty main album releases, all of which are single albums, apart from *Songs in the Key of Life*, which was released as a double album with a bonus four-track EP.

*Ray Charles* was a pioneer of soul music, integrating R&B, gospel, pop, and country to create hits like "Unchain My Heart," "Hit the Road Jack" and "Georgia on My Mind." *A blind genius*, he is considered one of the greatest artists of all time.

## *Examples of maximizing the creative potential of the human mind*

I thought it was necessary to pay homage to some of the world's greatest examples of maximizing the creative potential of the human mind in order to illustrate the difference between *wishing* for a thing and *being ready to receive it*, although you are not ready for a thing until you *believe* you can acquire it.

The state of mind must be *belief*, not mere hope or wish. Open-mindedness is essential for *belief*. Closed minds do not inspire faith, courage, nor belief.

Procrastination is defined as the avoidance of doing a task that needs to be accomplished. It could be further stated as a habitual or intentional delay of starting or finishing a task despite its negative consequences.

For this very important reason,

> Wanting something is not enough. You must hunger for it. Your motivation must be absolutely compelling in order to overcome the obstacles that will invariably come your way. (Les Brown)

His point is that "no one rises to low expectations."

# GREAT THINKING

Yet in spite of all this wisdom I've compiled from others, there is *tension* between the *ideal* and *reality*. The ideal is a model of something flawless, faultless, perfect, or without equal. As an adjective, *ideal* describes an ultimate standard for excellence or something that exists only as an idea.

On the other hand, reality is the sum or aggregate of all that is real or existent as opposed to that which is merely imaginary. The term is also used to refer to the ontological status of things, indicating their existence.

I noticed that in me, this tension between the ideal and reality surfaces between how things ought to be, how I want them to be, and how they really are.

Let's say the distance between the *ideal* and the *reality* is what determines the level of mental and emotional disappointment we frequently experience when our hope is disappointed or expectations are unfulfilled.

*Ideal* things might exist only in the imagination. It's desirable and perfect but not likely to become *reality* unless we initiate the correct exchanges.

The reason an ideal or an idea may not become reality is because we may fail to base them in effort, substance, or confirmable proofs.

It is this failure to substantiate an ideal that allows it to become a mental illusion. This happens many times because of the *risk* of losing the misery you may be accustomed to having.

Now let's rephrase the definition: "Things *ideal* exist only in the imagination *unless preparation happens*!" This is because preparation is a necessary key!

That's why thought or thinking preparation is necessary! Preparation is the bridge between wishing and knowing or *wishing* I could have something and *knowing* I can have something.

It has been said, "When you are 100 percent sure, you're too late." So don't wait until you're sure before you get started in the direction of your desire.

Today, you must settle that to live a life of *faith* will require you to take risks. Taking risks demands more time thinking than doing.

It is my constant observation that

> Those who commit to duty before thinking usually spend the majority of their lives fulfilling someone else ideas, dreams or imaginations. Those who commit to thinking before duty usually create the house, car, and industry for themselves and the non-thinkers abode.

*Also remember*, the cutting edge is not in the middle. In order to have or do anything significant or to build anything to last, you must take some *risk*, which makes it important to *prepare* for the *unexpected*.

Great preparation requires great thinking and planning. This is why you must be willing to set goals to keep yourself in compliance with progress and growth.

*Goals* demand from each of us the constant exercise of our thinking faculty.

Big-picture thinking and prioritized planning is the first two keys to success.

Former president Abraham Lincoln explained it best.

> Give me six hours to chop down a tree and
> I will spend the first four sharpening the axe.
> (Abraham Lincoln)

# *Peter's* Great *Discovery*
## Step out the Boat

In my lectures, I frequently refer to Peter's willingness to challenge the forces that be by stepping out of the boat of safety into the waters of uncertainty.

In testing his righteous yearnings to duplicate Jesus, his teacher walking on the water, he discovered something that the other eleven disciples did not risk—first, that he was able to tap into the existence of a power that was already there, in existence, but not initiated and, second, that the possibility of God's productive power is made possible by our believing whatever He says to us and acting on it.

I have discovered that one reason God's thoughts toward me are as the sands of the seashore is because life is lived in increments—one second, minute, hour, or day at a time.

Learning how to use these increments as fractional investments into the discovery of my unique potential continues to somehow help me unveil and fulfill ultimately my purpose for being.

Every day I awake on planet Earth, God affords me two brand-new privileges—time and choice! The way I value and use these two ultimately determines the nature of the gift I give to myself, which is chance! In other words, each new day, God gives us *time* to make *choices* that will determine the type and quality of *chances* we will give ourselves.

In the Gospel of Matthew 14:29, it says, "And when Peter had come down out of the boat, he walked on the water to go to Jesus."

Here, Peter was willing to take the *risk* of walking on the water to go to Jesus. And he succeeded until, in the passionate heat of the moment, he failed to *anticipate* the *unexpected* in order to continue to walk on the water to fully accomplish his objective for leaving the boat. However, he was willing to make something of himself.

Peter did not fail to *try*; he simply failed to finish. In his failure to finish, Jesus demonstrated how to review the occasion as an opportunity to do risk management instead of overthink his sinking. Notice: "And immediately Jesus stretched out His hand and caught him, and said to him, 'O you of little faith, *why did you doubt?*'"

In other words, you were doing so well, but when you learn *why* you started doubting or *what* initiated your doubt, you will remember *how* to finish what you start.

In faith systems, how you start often determines how you'll finish. If you start in faith, you must remain undistracted by sight because things you *see* may subdue or subvert your ability to continue believing you'll succeed.

*Preparation* is *a key* to *success*.

*Preparation* allows you the great privilege of anticipation by reviewing your endeavors in advance (like an architect who measures and weighs in the planning phase) before getting started.

Four risk factors:

1. Many times, we fail to understand that *risk* actually determines the *value* a person places on a thing or the *benefit* of accomplishing a *goal*.
2. The more *value* I place on the goal or the thing I desire, the more likely I am willing to take the *risk*.
3. The less *value* it holds, the less likely we are to take the *risk*. An example of how *risk* factors can be seen was when Rosa Parks discovered her rights as an individual, she decided to take her seat and refuse to move to the back of the bus. Her *rights* were *valuable* to her!
4. *Here*, value-driven *desire* is the *fuel* to persistence that enables a person to hurdle over *risk* when they are factored in as part of the process.

Many times, the difference between those who are successful and those who fail may be that successful people keep applying themselves even when the *risks* are high.

They develop a *routine* through persistence that turns into *momentum* by majoring in the *possibilities*, not the *risk*.

But on the other hand, those who *fail* usually stop applying themselves whenever *risk* surfaces because they major in the risk instead of the *possibilities*.

Booker T. (Taliaferro) Washington—a dominant leader in the African American community who served as an American educator, author, orator, and adviser to presidents of the United States between 1890 and 1915—is quoted as saying, "Success is to be measured not so much by the position that one has reached in life as by the *obstacles* which he has overcome."

# *The Power of Thought*
## *You* Need to *Educate* Yourself

The power of thought is phenomenally incredible. The Bible opens with the dynamic use of this magnificent power on display by featuring God as the thinking source that recreated the social stratum as it appeared to have become void and chaotic. As a result of His sovereign omniscience, He demonstrates to mankind for all ages to come the appropriate way to influence whole-life reconstruction and reconciliation over chaos caused by adversarial forces.

The power of *thought* is so vigorously forceful and enterprising that every time you *think*, you are emitting a generously one-of-a-kind electromagnetic unit into the universe. Each *thought* is your personal vibration being emitted into the environment that belongs solely to you.

Throughout the book of Proverbs, Solomon emphasizes the importance of *thinking* and the priority it should be given over activities and behaviors. It was profoundly clear to him that "understanding (spiritual insight) is a [refreshing and boundless] wellspring of life to those who have it."

Otherwise, those without it might spend their lives in folly and recklessness because of a lack of understanding what's most important. Notice his advice in Proverbs 13:3: "The one who guards his mouth [*thinking* before he speaks] protects his life; The one who opens his lips wide [and chatters without thinking] comes to ruin."

He constantly compelled men to "ponder, consider well and watch carefully the path of your feet, and let all your ways will be established, steadfast and sure" (Proverbs 4:26).

# GREAT THINKING

In other words, you must be committed to ponder-think, consider-think, and watch carefully-think in order to pay the price for your own existence.

Paul, the great apostle of the New Testament, made it abundantly clear that we have to be aware of our thoughts because they are powerful cosmic waves in the universal galaxy of energy we live in, and the proper exchanges ensure us of God's peace in our lives.

Notice how he emphasized the priority and preeminence of right thinking in Philippians 4:8–9.

> Finally, believers, whatever is true, whatever is honorable and worthy of respect, whatever is right and confirmed by God's word, whatever is pure and wholesome, whatever is lovely and brings peace, whatever is admirable and of good repute; if there is any excellence, if there is anything worthy of praise, think continually on these things [center your mind on them, and implant them in your heart]. The things which you have learned and received and heard and seen in me, practice these things [in daily life], and the God [who is the source] of peace and well-being will be with you.

Clearly, apart from Spirit, the most potent form of energy is thought because thought-waves are cosmic waves penetrating through time and space.

While looking through my journal, I stumbled across this quote accredited to both Lao Tzu and Ralph Waldo Emerson. I first heard this quote during an impartation by Dr. Creflo A. Dollar in our annual "Eagles Gathering," which establishes the importance of being consciously aware of our thinking.

> Watch your thoughts, they become *words*.
> Watch your words, they become *actions*.
> Watch your actions, they become *habits*.

> Watch your habits, they become your *character*.
> Watch your character, it becomes your *destiny*.

This quote is particularly important because it demonstrates the flow of the creative process and power of *life* from *thoughts* to *destiny*.

In the Old Testament, God impressed upon both Moses and Joshua the importance of thinking and its dynamically strategic influence upon creativity in their personal lives and among their families.

He revealed this principle to Moses in Deuteronomy chapter 6 and to Joshua in chapter 1, verses 7 to 9. He also revealed to David in the first Psalm verses 1 to 3 the method for controlling our thinking and the fact that we are able to control our thoughts.

This method is described as the *inculcation principle*.

*Inculcation* is the instilling of knowledge or values from God's Words in someone usually by repetition. To inculcate is to instill or impress an idea on someone.

Through Moses, the Hebrews revered this method of teaching because God instructed them to constantly convey His promises to each generation by repeating them to their children and families, hoping it will sink in.

Notice:

> Memorize His laws and tell them to your children over and over again. Talk about them all the time, whether you're at home or walking along the road or going to bed at night, or getting up in the morning. Write down copies and tie them to your wrists and foreheads to help you obey them. Write these laws on the door frames of your homes and on your town gates. (Deuteronomy 6:6–9 CEV)

It is also clearly etched in the ink of Holy Writ that we can use our minds to practice the process of thinking and we can make ourselves think thoughts regarding what we want to be or have.

# GREAT THINKING

In Wallace D. Wattles's book *The Science of Getting Rich*, a central part of the book is about the power of thought. The statement I'm particularly fond of hits the bull's-eye on the target of my research because it affirms most of my beliefs from the Holy Scriptures regarding *faith* and the *mind*.

Notice:

> To think what you want to think is to think *truth regardless of appearances.* To think according to appearances is easy. To *think truth regardless of appearances* is laborious and requires the expenditure of more power than any other work you have to perform.

Paul, the apostle, said in his second letter to the church, "For we walk by faith, not by sight [living our lives in a manner consistent with our confident belief in God's promises]" (2 Corinthians 5:7 AMP).

In his letter to the Hebrews, the apostle wrote to explain *faith*.

> Now *faith* is the assurance (title deed, confirmation) of things hoped for (divinely guaranteed), and the *evidence* of things *not seen* [the conviction of their reality—*faith* comprehends as fact *What cannot be* experienced by the *physical senses*]. For by this [kind of] faith the men of old gained [divine] approval.
>
> By faith [that is, with an inherent trust and enduring confidence in the power, wisdom and goodness of God] we understand that the worlds (universe, ages) were framed and created [formed, put in order, and equipped for their intended purpose] by the word of God, so that what is *seen* was *not made* out *of* things which are *visible.* (Hebrews 11:1–3 AMP)

Clearly we can choose to think as an optimist and have a *positive* view on life. Or we can choose to think as a pessimist and have a *negative* view on life.

Winston Churchill is quoted as saying, "A pessimist sees the difficulty in every opportunity; an optimist sees the opportunity in every difficulty."

Churchill also stated, "Difficulties mastered are opportunities won. For myself I am an optimist—it does not seem to be much use being anything else."

Norman Vincent Peale—an American minister and author known for his work in popularizing the concept of positive thinking, especially through his best-selling book *The Power of Positive Thinking*—is quoted as saying, "Our happiness depends on the habit of mind we cultivate."

Peale believed that

> When you expect the best, you release a magnetic force in your mind which by a law of attraction tends to bring the best to you. If you decide to really achieve something in your life—you will. It's all a matter of how you *think* about yourself and what you *think* you are capable of. The power of *thought* is incredible. You can work wonders with the power of thought. Through the instrumentality of thought, you acquire creative power.

# *Mind* Explorations and Capabilities

We all constantly feel frustrations and pressures as we find ourselves unable to live up to our personal expectations. So many times, we can't seem to shake the old bad habits or health problems that have controlled us in the past and prevented us from moving ahead to acquire new beneficial forms of self-discipline.

In this book, I want to prove that significant, even dramatic, change is possible! I used an analysis comparing neurophysiologists' writings with the scriptural documents written by the apostles because they both confirm that *change* is possible.

Now you, like so many others, may be wondering, *How?* Let me suggest to you that God has not left us without definitive instructions for influencing dynamic change in your life. By learning to properly meditate through Scripture, prayer, and other faith techniques, you can set the stage for important *mind-* and *habit*-altering *thinking exchanges.* Furthermore, you will be able to break free into a new way of life, where you are maximizing your innermost inherent capabilities.

I will discuss in the following pages how you can increase your chances to

* succeed with building self-esteem,
* strengthen your self-discipline,
* achieve difficult goals and objectives,
* support and expand your spiritual life, and
* much more.

Harvard professor Herbert Benson, MD, is one of the most leading authorities on stress and the mind's ability to influence health.

He teaches a practical formula in which recent studies prove that the right and left sides of the brain govern very different modes of thinking—logical thought from the left side and intuitive thought from the right. Because the dominant left side of the brain often overrules creative and corrective impulses sent by the right, we tend to repeat old habits and cling to old behaviors, even those we genuinely want to change.

According to Benson, the very way our brains are constructed is often what keeps us at cross purposes with aspirations for personal growth and renewal, but this doesn't have to become a permanent condition.

Benson shows in his book, *Your Maximum Mind*, that our thought patterns can be beneficially "rewired" into more desirable pathways after periods of deep calm. Elicitation of the relaxation response, which induces such a state, is therefore critical as the first step in any self-help program, and Dr. Benson reviews it here. But in *Your Maximum Mind*, he goes further to describe an important second step that brings into reach for the first time the enormous potential of *whole-brain thinking*.

Through this study, he identified several methods for achieving some specific goals:

1. A stronger will and enhanced results for those in any self-help or health regiment
2. Deeper insights into the spirituality of those grappling with religious convictions
3. Better performance and more enjoyment for those in athletic training
4. Increased on-the-job performance

During my experiment with the principle of the maximum mind, I was actually able to utilize more power from my own unique capabilities. Although it requires self-discipline, the principle shows you how to tap into and more fully exercise your own strengths easily and effectively.

Physiologists state that over the years of your life, you develop what they describe as "circuits" and "channels" of fault in your brain. These are physical pathways that control the way you think; the way you act; and, often, the way you feel. Also at times, these pathways or habits become so fixed that they turn into what they call *wiring*. In other words, the circuits or channels become so deeply ingrained that it seems almost impossible to transform them.

By *comparison*, Paul, in 2 Corinthians 10:3–5, calls these fixed, deeply ingrained "circuits" and "channels" of fault "strongholds." Verse 5 says,

> [Inasmuch as we] refute arguments and theories and reasonings and every proud and lofty thing that sets itself up against the [true] knowledge of God; and we lead every thought and purpose away captive into the obedience of Christ (the Messiah, the Anointed One). (AMP)

Neurophysiologists like Drs. Roger Sperry and Michael S. Gazzaniga have been investigating the so-called "split brain" phenomena involving the activities of the left and right hemispheres of the brain. Among other things, they have demonstrated that the left hemisphere of the brain is largely responsible for controlling much of the analytical, inferential, and language-related skills and thinking processes. The right hemisphere is the area in which much of the intuitive, artistic, and creative thinking resides.

Consider, for example, the question of how you can change a bad habit or acquire a new skill. By various logical but often inaccurate inferences, your left brain may in effect "tell" you that certain beneficial changes in your personality, skills, and habits are impossible. And despite the inaccuracies, you will believe what you're "hearing" internally. Why? Because more often than not, there will be little internal argument or opposition from your right hemisphere.

In very practical terms, then, it's largely the established circuits of the left side of our brain that are telling us we can't change our way of living nor our bad habits because they are forever. We're just made in a certain way, and we have to live with that fact. But that's simply not true!

It's important to note here that the references of neurophysiologists differ from apostolic scriptural explanations regarding "split brain" and "mind" phenomena. The first is largely interpreted by the effects of the channels of change.

# The Channels of Change

Studies prove that the habits, thought patterns, and attitudes that influence the way you think and behave are not etched in some gray concrete in your head. On the contrary, your mind and mine are malleable, capable of being molded into new shapes and forms like some exquisite living sculpture.

Neurophysiologists believe the left hemisphere of the brain is as essential and important as it is in helping us pursue meaningful, effective lives; it tends to get in the way of our efforts to change ourselves. In a sense, the left brain may act as a kind of rigid intellectual guardian that interferes with any moves we make to change our habits and personal disciplines for the better.

They strongly believe it is not that the left hemisphere is inherently evil or some sort of enemy that we need to engage in Mortal Kombat. Rather, the left side has just been conditioned into thinking that certain things are good for us as human beings when in fact, those things may really be detrimental to our growth and well-being.

While on the other hand, Paul and the other the apostles are convinced that this internal strife demands "mind renewal" using the Word of God because it infers conflict between grace and corruption.

One example of how the left brain guards its domain can be found in a theory known in the psychological profession as "cognitive dissonance."

This is the concept put forth by the pioneering social psychologist Dr. Leon Festinger that when a belief and a behavior are in conflict, the *belief* must change to fit the *behavior* or the behavior must change to conform to the belief. The left brain, upon confronting a belief-related conflict, is driven to make sense of it to bring our values and actions into some sort of consistency. Usually, according to his studies, it's the belief that does the changing.

One experiment that helped establish this conclusion involved students who were asked how they felt about cheating. Some of them said they felt it was a very bad thing, while others responded, in effect, "Gee, it's not really so bad, is it?"

Subsequently, all the students were given an examination in which it was very easy to cheat in a way that seemed undetectable. In fact, the researchers could determine who was cheating and who wasn't.

Those conducting the study found that even though many had initially said they thought cheating was bad, they did in fact cheat when given an easy opportunity. Next, after the test was finished, all the students were again asking how they felt about cheating.

The results? Those who had initially felt cheating was bad but had actually engaged in cheating now said they felt cheating wasn't so bad. In other words, the students' values and actions ended up conforming more with one another when they were confronted with having to deal with this issue of cheating directly.

In this situation, the left brain stepped in and tried to make sense out of the difficult challenge facing the students. Through a process of rationalization, the students who cheated in violation of their anti-cheating beliefs found reasons to change their values. They seemed to decide that what they had done wasn't so bad. Furthermore, it would appear, they reasoned, that "everybody cheats in this sort of situation, so I may as well do the same. I may not be perfect, but I'm still a good person."

The value systems of some students fall captive to the needs of the left brain to maintain logical consistency. This is just one instance of a much more pervasive problem.

The left brain can imprison us with problems like phobias in much the same way. Suppose, for example, you are standing in a supermarket line with an unpleasant crowd pushing in and around you and you develop a stomach pain. To make things worse, that stomach pain stays with you, and you become ill that evening.

It is quite possible that the left side of your brain, inferring a relationship between the pain and the supermarket lines, may give you the message "I shouldn't stand in supermarket lines, and if I do, the experience is going to be unpleasant." In fact, this conclusion may be completely erroneous.

There may be no relationship between your standing in the supermarket line and that stomach pain, but if your left-brain hemispheric activity somehow leads you to that conclusion, you could develop a fear of supermarket lines.

Many phobias can develop this way and may be the direct result of the interpretations and inferences that the left hemisphere gives to the circumstances and feelings that we are experiencing.

Those confronted by such phobias, however, are not going to be enslaved forever by such fears.

In other words, the brain really is capable of adapting and overcoming many of these emotional shackles that bind us. But in physical terms, how does this occur?

# How Mental Transformation Occurs

In brief, to maximize when one's *mind* or mental capacity may work like this—when we change our patterns of thinking and acting—the brain cells begin to establish additional connections or new wirings.

These new connections then communicate in fresh ways with other cells, and before long, the pathways or wirings that kept the phobia or other habit you like were all replaced or altered each time you decide you're going to learn to do something different as you take lessons and spend time practicing. During this process, brain cells that control this particular skill establish new connections that enable you to function according to your new desires.

So it is with the *thinking process.*

If you don't make any effort to change your way of thinking or develop new skills or disciplines, the brain cells never establish the requisite new connections or patterns. Similarly, if you don't work to maintain the new patterns and physical skills, they will diminish. It's clearly a case, as far as your brain is concerned, of "use it or lose it."

Aiding and underlying this process of change in the brain is the basic fact that the brain is a malleable, adaptable organ. The nervous system, including our mental powers, is not immutable, which means it's not unchangeable, with habits, thought patterns, and skills permanently fixed.

So from this premise, there is absolutely no reason you can't make considerable progress by using the success principal in Joshua chapter 1 verse 8. A key to this change is to learn to eliminate the unhealthy dictatorship of the left side of your brain and put both hemispheres of your brain in greater harmony. Notice God's instructions to Joshua: "Keep this Book of the Law always on your lips; *med-*

*itate* on it day and night, so that you may be careful to do everything written in it. Then you will be prosperous and successful."

*Meditation* is the physiological door that will open the way for you to change your thought patterns and your life.

When you get aroused, anxious, or angry at a particular challenge or difficult situation, your body secretes certain hormones called catecholamines that "rev you up." They prepare you to deal quickly and decisively with a perceived threat.

## The "Faith" Factor

Probably the most powerful major factor in enabling you to change your brain and your life, one which I have briefly alluded to before, is the intensity of your personal belief system.

Dr. Herbert Benson, MD, author of *Your Maximum Mind*, says,

> The brain responds and changes when deep personal belief and conviction take hold in our lives. Our beliefs and convictions are part of our thoughts and thus part of our brains. When we think or act out of a deep conviction, we are tapping into an already existing "brain wiring." As a result, we feel that what we're doing is true and correct; we feel comfortable operating on the foundation of deeply held convictions.
>
> Under the circumstances, new thought patterns and actions can develop much more readily. The tracks are, if you will, already greased and the new patterns more easily established. The neurotransmitters in the cells may thus transmit new messages more easily, and this, in turn, facilitates the development of the newer thought processes, skills, and disciplines.

*Belief* often remains a primary driving and enhancing force in developing these new pathways, grooves, and wirings in the brain. A good illustration of the power of belief in mind-body interactions in medical research involves what is known as the "placebo effect."

A placebo is anything that seems to be a "real" medical treatment but isn't. It could be a pill, a shot, or some other type of "fake" treatment. What all placebos have in common is that they do not contain an active substance meant to affect health.

This phenomenon has three components: beliefs and expectations on the part of a patient or person being healed; beliefs and expectations of the doctor, health professional, or healer; and beliefs and expectations inherent in the relationship of health professional to patient or healer to patient.

To explore the power of the patients' beliefs, research and study was done with one group of women who were suffering from nausea and vomiting during pregnancy.

First, the women were asked to swallow small intragastric balloons, which measured their stomach contractions. The balloons detected characteristic ways of nausea and vomiting. Then they were given a substance that, they were told, would stop the vomiting and nausea. In fact, they were given syrup of ipecac, a medication often used to cause vomiting.

The results in this case determined that their *belief* triumphed over physical forces and medicine because they believed they were getting anti-nausea medication. For many of the women, nausea and vomiting disappeared; and as measured in the balloon, their stomach contractions also returned to normal. Here we have a situation where the belief in a substance actually reversed the physiological action of the drug. The wiring of the brain was more powerful than the drug.

Sometimes, acute fear or induced terror causes a very large amount of stress-related chemical from which one can have devastating physical effects. The release of too much of this substance may trigger a series of biochemical steps that end in massive changes in the heart muscle and death.

One scientific study shows that eleven of fifteen subjects who were victims of physical assault and died as a result of the attacks did not sustain any internal injuries according to the autopsies. Instead, they have suffered a condition known as myofibrillar degeneration or a type of heart-muscle damage.

This could be the same process by which voodoo death occurs in certain primitive societies. There, a curse may be pronounced on an individual by a powerful medicine man. The victim often dies quickly afterward. His belief that he's going to die kills him more than anything else. Similarly, the people who died during mugging attacks expired from the results of their belief in the possible harm from the attack rather than from the attack itself.

Other studies have shown that the belief of the physician or healer is also extremely important.

One group of physicians working in conjunction with a drug company was given the same generic tranquilizer but under two different brand names, only one of which was from their company. They were then asked to test the two brands.

The results showed that the substance that was labeled as being produced by their own company did better than the other brand, even though there was no difference between the two substances except their names. In short, it was the belief of the physicians in their own product that seemed to make the difference in the way the product worked on patients.

An example of the third element of the placebo effect, the power of the doctor-patient relationship, involves a study that was conducted at Massachusetts General Hospital with two similar groups of patients who were about to undergo surgery. They were approached by an anesthetist in two different ways. He dealt with one group of patients in a rather cursory fashion. With the other group, the same anesthetist behaved in a much warmer, more sympathetic fashion. He sat down on the bed; explained in detail what was going to occur in the operation; described the amount and type of pain to be expected; and, in general, was extremely supportive. He developed a solid doctor-patient relationship, and as a result, the patient's developed confidence and positive belief or faith in the physician.

Then all the patients went through their surgery and postsurgical procedures. All were allowed to receive as much pain-alleviating medication as they requested. During this phase, all were treated by hospital personnel who either did not know to which group the patient belonged or who were unaware that the test was being conducted.

After the study was completed, the investigators found that the patients who have been treated in a warm and sympathetic manner asked for half as much pain medication as the other group. Also, the ones who had enjoyed the warm doctor-patient relationship were discharged from the hospital, on average, 2.7 days sooner than the other group.

In each of the situations, the power of belief on healing is evident. The *mind* begins to work independently of medication and other factors and, in effect, takes on a life of its own in influencing bodily reactions. In short, *beliefs* seem capable of enhancing and transforming the mind with dramatic results.

When comparing this same phenomenon from a more theological or spiritual perspective, *beliefs* are vitally essential to the experience of faith.

Each of us should be concerned about whether we are building our beliefs on the proper life foundation by applying God's confirmable truths that give us the correct way to live.

A phrase that you will hear repeated throughout my messages is found in Proverbs 16:25: "There is a way that seems right to a man, but ends in multiple ways of death."

Now let's begin this journey of close examination together.

First, notice the implication of Psalm 11:3: "If the foundations are destroyed. What can the righteous do?" We know that the righteous are those who have submitted their lives to God's way of doing and being right.

But what is a foundation, and why is it important to have right foundational beliefs? Or to make this more relevant, why do you do what you do? And who or what influences the direction of your life?

Are you living in a self-defeating cycle of frustrations and chaos? Is it good to impress and appease others at the expense of your personal peace and power? Lastly, who told you or what makes you think you've discovered the appropriate way to live?

*Webster* defines a *foundation* as the base on which something rests or the basis for which something exists, specifically the supporting part of a wall, house, relationship, system, reality, etc., and at least partially underground the fundamental principle on which something is founded.

Greek nouns *themelios* or *themelion* denotes a thing, a standard, a principle or a system upon which something is built. It is used as a noun with *lithos*: a stone. This implies that our beliefs should be constructed on the right foundation.

Herein lies the acid test to determine if our practices and habits are correctly established on the correct foundation.

> If an *action* or *reaction* in which you engage constantly leaves you without internal *peace* or *rest*, you need to examine it or weigh it against the *truth*.

What's happening to you may not be the problem, but how you *believe* you should handle it may be in need of change! Many times we handle our affairs according to what *seems* right to us instead of what *is* appropriate (or the standard) for a situation.

Here is something you should always remember: that which we consider as *normal* usually determines the importance we place on it because our definition of *normalcy* was probably drafted and shaped from the experiences of our developmental years, which may or may not have included God.

Things that are important to us are important because they have become our *standards* that impact the way we believe and the things in which we believe.

Our *beliefs* reside in our conscience, which is the place where "strongholds" are erected that form our deep-seated convictions and mindsets.

Ultimately, our *convictions*, referred to by *Webster* as "strong beliefs or opinions," are the forces that work together to drive our *responses*.

This process influences our behaviors regardless of whether they are right or wrong, which in essence is the single reason the standard for all of our operations needs to be tested against the "*truth*" of God's Word.

If you are, in any way, like I was before I began this journey, testing your *beliefs* and *practices* against "truth" will divinely inspire you. You might see changes in your *thought* processes and habits that have developed over your life span.

Whenever our convictions drive our responses, we are usually inflexible about the position we take whether it is correct or not. The problem is that we may have settled with the wrong frame of mind. The way we handle our personal issues and other people will, to a great extent, determine the quality, happiness, and success of our lives. Give yourself time and space to *think*!

## Get Initiated

To those who have not been schooled in the working principles of the human mind, these instructions may appear impractical.

The initiated *mind* houses a *grace* that calls for no hard labor. It calls for no hard sacrifice. It does not require one to become ridiculous or credulous. It handles principles that call for no great amount of education. But the successful application of the principles does call for sufficient imagination to enable you, as an individual, to see and to understand that becoming accomplished cannot be left to chance, good fortune, nor luck.

For this reason, God compels us to "walk and regulate our affairs by faith, not by sight." If you have unbelief, which many times results from logical facts, it can stop needed change and supernatural things from manifesting in your life. In this, unbelief is a *thought-barrier* that subjects a person to whatever reality they conceive or imagine to be true.

You must realize that to succeed in accomplishing your aspirations along with belief, a certain amount of dreaming, hoping, wishing, desiring, and planning is required before you succeed in your desires.

Through the power of faith, your belief is the greatest potential power in the world. No greater person has ever been on the earth than our Savior Jesus. His successful adventure taught us that *belief* is to *faith* what *water* is to *ice*.

# GREAT THINKING

## *Belief is to faith what water is to ice*

Without belief, there's absolutely *no* action, manifestation, or material substance that can be derived from faith.

In order to move into possibilities in spite of your difficulties, your state of mind must be "belief." Like an anonymous person once said, "I've decided I'd rather believe for something *great* and get half of it than believe for nothing and get *all* of it."

Don't allow any type of experience you've had consistently nor any setback you've encountered recently to block your ability to trust God by believing His Word.

God's Word must take precedence and final authority over everything else in life. In Mark 9:23, Jesus said, "All things are possible to *believers.*"

That's because *beliefs are gateways to godly possibilities in your life.*

If you don't believe, faith will not produce nor manufacture manifestation in your life. In other words, unbelief cancels manifestation!

Let's look at Mark 6:1–6,

> Then He went out from there and came to His own country, and His disciples followed Him. And when the Sabbath had come, He began to teach in the synagogue. And many hearing Him were astonished, saying, "Where did this Man get these things? And what wisdom is this which is given to Him, that such mighty works are performed by His hands! Is this not the carpenter, the Son of Mary, and brother of James, Joses, Judas, and Simon? And are not His sisters here with us?" So they were offended at Him. But Jesus said to them, "A prophet is not without honor except in his own country, among his own relatives, and in his own house."

Two pivotal verses:

> Now *He* could do no *mighty work there*, except that He laid His hands on a few sick people and healed them. And *He marveled* because of their *unbelief.* Then He went about the villages in a circuit, *teaching.*

He demonstrated teaching as the cure for unbelief.

My ultimate goal for selecting this story is to educate and enlighten you as *believers* to change by reshaping your sense of being and concept of having—in other words, how you see yourself!

What makes this important is that I fully embrace the truth that my *beliefs* are my *reality*!

Remember, if you don't believe, grace will not produce nor manufacture manifestation in your life because *unbelief* cancels manifestation!

In selecting this account, I realized that Christ Himself was condemned by His own countrymen, the citizens of Nazareth, because He was one of them and they knew Him since youth. At least, they thought they knew His original design and purpose but refused to allow themselves to benefit from His dissimilarity.

It's important to realize that people who say they know you may not always esteem or appeal to the most important characteristics about you, especially your unique gifts, skills, and abilities because they make you a viable asset to society in ways that might exceed them.

We also discovered in this text that you may never meet severer critics than those who say they know you from youth.

My last point of emphasis is, *how* you *see* God determines how you talk to God, how you relate to Him, how frequent you solicit His advice or direction, and especially how much stock you put in His Word.

All behavior is the offspring of a belief system that shows what we really *think* about God, things, and people, which is why I often say, "You can live a lifetime with a *lie*. The *difference* in people is who they've chosen to trust and what they are willing to permit."

We create belief systems to create comfort or change in our personal lives. As indicated here, it will be based upon our own perception or the dictations of others.

Notice how the people of His own country allowed themselves to be influenced against Him, even though He was God's agency of hope and change. They were vulnerable simply because He did not cater to their norms. He also had a more superior and significant purpose than they'd ever witnessed, so they refused to receive Him as God's gift to them.

This is why what's in the *word* must be in your *heart* and what's in your *heart* will become the manifestation of your *life*!

The devil knows something that the majority of the people in our society do not. That's why he works so hard to "blind the minds of unbelievers." He constantly infiltrates their minds with so many issues and challenges that they never get a chance to respond to the spirit of grace and all its vast substances.

For this reason, God revealed through the prophet, "My people are destroyed for a lack of knowledge."

Never in the history of the world has there been so great an opportunity for practical dreamers as now. Faith in God makes all things possible.

# The *Distinction* between the *Mind* and the *Brain*

After putting so many hours in research to clarify and establish the importance of *thinking*, I realized that this research would not be complete if I failed to distinguish the difference between the mind and the human brain.

One of the most puzzling and mysterious issues that faces those doing brain research is the distinction between the mind and the brain. Is the mind the same as the brain? Or is the mind somehow made up of features that transcend the physical makeup of the brain?

There's been considerable discussion about this point over the years. The Bible concordance lists 615 occurrences relative to the *mind*. Some argue that our minds are the sum total of our brain's physical capabilities, nothing more and nothing less. But Sir John Eccles, who won the Nobel Prize for medicine in 1963, has rejected such a mechanistic view of man's thinking processes. He doesn't think that the power of the mind rests exclusively in nerve cells, dendrites, synapses, and neurotransmitters. Rather, he states,

> I believe that there is a fundamental mystery in my existence, transcending any biological account of the development of my body (including my brain) with its genetic inheritance and it's evolutionary origin.

In a similar vein, the famous Canadian neurosurgeon, Wilder Penfield, wrote in the *Mystery of the Mind* that the workings of the mind will probably always be impossible to explain simply on the basis of electrical or chemical action in the brain and nervous system. "The *mind* is independent of the brain," he declared. "The brain is a computer, but it is programmed by something that is outside itself, the *mind*."

Is it possible to define the *mind*?

In scientific terms, we simply can't be definitive. The mind certainly resides by and large in the brain. In many ways, it also seems to go beyond individual brain components. Religious groups have long recognized this transcendent feature of our consciousness as they use terms like the *human spirit* or *similar metaphysical language*. There is a link between religious insight and this phenomenon of the mind, which somehow seems to transcend the physical.

In this regard, it's interesting to me that meditation, with all its physiological and spiritual benefits, has, most often and effectively, been elicited through forms of prayer, which is an ability of human beings given by God to break through ingrained habits and thought patterns and transform lives.

Caroline Leaf, PhD, BSc, is a communication pathologist and cognitive neuroscientist specializing in cognitive and metacognitive neuropsychology. She received her masters and PhD in communication pathology, as well as a BSc in logopedics from the University of Cape Town and the University of Pretoria in South Africa. During her years in clinical practice and her work with thousands of underprivileged teachers and students in her home country of South Africa and in the USA, she developed a theory about how we think, build memory, and learn (called the geodesic information processing theory). Leaf is the author of *Switch on Your Brain*; *Think, Learn, Succeed*; *Think and Eat Yourself Smart*; and *Cleaning Up Your Mental Mess*.

Her elaborate studies for over thirty years have led her to conclude what I think is reflected clearly in the holy scriptures. My appreciation of her works inspires me to quote a few of her statements to express my belief about this distinction.

First,

> The mind works through the brain but is separate from the brain. For many people, the mind and brain are interchangeable. They use

one word or the other to talk about the same thing: the organ in our skull that we use to think. However, the mind and brain are actually two very different, but interconnected, entities.

Second,

> The mind is separate, yet inseparable from, the brain. The mind uses the brain, and the brain responds to the mind. The mind also changes the brain. People choose their actions—their brains do not force them to do anything. Yes, there would be no conscious experience without the brain, but experience cannot be reduced to the brain's actions.

Third,

> The mind is energy, and it generates energy through thinking, feeling, and choosing. It is our aliveness, without which, the physical brain and body would be useless. That means we are our mind, and mind-in-action is how we generate energy in the brain.

Fourth,

> When we generate this mind energy through thinking, feeling, and choosing, we build thoughts, which are physical structures in our brain made of proteins. This building of thoughts creates structural changes in the brain, called neuroplasticity.

She stated that during her recent clinical trials, they saw how energy in the brain changed as the subject was thinking, stimulating neuroplasticity. The brain was responding to the person's stream-of-consciousness and nonconscious activity.

Fifth,

> The mind is a stream of nonconscious and conscious activity when we're awake, and a stream of nonconscious activity when we're asleep. It's characterized by a triad of thinking, feeling, and choosing. When you think, you will feel, and when you think and feel, you will choose. These three aspects always work together. So how does this affect us? This essentially means each time the brain is stimulated by your mind, it responds in various ways—including neurochemical, genetic, and electromagnetic changes. This, in turn, grows and changes structures in the brain, building or wiring new physical thoughts. The brain is never the same because it changes with every experience you have, every moment of every day.

Sixth,

> In sum: Your mind is how you, uniquely, experience life. It's responsible for how you think, feel, and choose. And your physical brain merely responds to these unique experiences. Knowing your mind and brain are separate puts you in the control seat because you can learn to manage your thoughts and actions. Ultimately, it means you can choose what you build into your brain and how you choose to change what's already built in. When you learn how to manage your mind, you can make feelings of depression, stress, anger, and anxiety work for you instead of against you. You can bring balance back into your brain and life.

As children of God, we must commit ourselves to read, study, meditate, and confess the Word of God until we can consciously apprehend His will through a transformed life, which will only result from a renewed mind. This we do by submitting to the guidance of the Holy Spirit while remaining constant in prayer. Romans 12:1, 2 implies that until we are transformed by renewing our minds, we cannot prove the good, acceptable, and perfect will of God. It is in this light Paul attempts to draw us to the revelation of the practical method he was led by the Holy Spirit to commit to in order to conceive properly the experience of living a transformed life.

I refer to this as "the principle of structured forgetting" or the "FRP" principle. Throughout Paul's letters, I noticed how constant he was in his pursuit of godliness as it related to his calling and purpose.

> Not that I have already attained, or am already perfected; but I press on, that I may lay hold of that for which Christ Jesus has also laid hold of me. Brethren, I do not count myself to have apprehended; but one thing I do, *forgetting* those things which are behind and *reaching* forward to those things which are ahead, I *press* toward the goal for the prize of the upward call of God in Christ Jesus.
>
> Therefore let us, as many as are mature, have this mind; and if in anything you think otherwise, God will reveal even this to you. (Philippians 3:12–15 NKJV)

The Amplified Bible brings further clarity to this divine revelation. Note,

> Brothers and sisters, I do not consider that I have made it my own yet; but one thing I do: forgetting what lies behind and reaching forward to what lies ahead, I press on toward the goal to win the [heavenly] prize of the upward call of

# GREAT THINKING

God in Christ Jesus. All of us who are mature [pursuing spiritual perfection] should have this attitude. And if in any respect you have a different attitude, that too God will make clear to you. (Philippians 3:13–15 AMP)

Here's a point you can't overlook.

After you accept Jesus into your life, your *mind* is to be regarded as the first place of alignment. This is so that you can begin to conceive or apprehend the spiritual work of grace done in your heart by the Holy Spirit, and as Paul said to the Ephesians,

> That the God of our Lord Jesus Christ, the Father of glory, may give to you the spirit of wisdom and revelation in the knowledge of Him, the eyes of your understanding being enlightened; That you may know what is the hope of His calling, what are the riches of the glory of His inheritance in the saints, and what is the exceeding greatness of His power toward us who believe, according to the working of His mighty power which He worked in Christ when He raised Him from the dead and seated Him at His right hand in the heavenly places, far above all principality and power and might and dominion, and every name that is named, not only in this age but also in that which is to come. And He put all things under His feet, and gave Him to be head over all things to the church, (Ephesians 1:17–22 NKJV)

Although this is a lot to apprehend or capture, you can accomplish it by the aid of the Holy Spirit. In Paul's first letter to the Corinthians, he wrote, "But as it is written: 'Eye has not seen, nor ear heard, Nor have entered into the heart of man The things which God has prepared for those who love Him.'"

*The implication is* "but God has revealed them to us through His Spirit (the Holy Spirit)."

Next, he exposes another one of the Spirit's purposes: "For the Spirit searches all things, yes, the deep things of God. For what man knows the things of a man except the spirit of the man which is in him? Even so no one knows the things of God except the Spirit of God."

Last, he reaffirms by summarizing with emphasis: "Now we have received, not the spirit of the world, but the Spirit who is from God, that we might *know the things* that have been freely given to us by God" (1 Corinthians 2:9–12 NKJV).

It is clear that the Holy Spirit wanted us to understand that this was the same method promised by Jesus in the Gospel of John.

Notice: "But the Comforter (Counselor, Helper, Intercessor, Advocate, Strengthener, Standby), the Holy Spirit, Whom the Father will send in My name [in My place, to represent Me and act on My behalf].

Here, the emphasis is "*He* will teach you all things. And *He* will cause you to recall [will remind you of, bring to your remembrance] everything I have told you" (John 14:26 AMP).

In Paul's second Epistle to the Corinthians, he explains the dynamic change of spirit that happens immediately during the experience of salvation. Note:

> Therefore, if anyone is in Christ, he is a new creation; old things have passed away; behold, all things have become new. Now all things are of God, who has reconciled us to Himself through Jesus Christ, and has given us the ministry of reconciliation. (2 Corinthians 5:17, 18 NKJV)

It must be clear that the born-again experience is the regeneration process that happens in your spirit by the Holy Spirit to redeem, resurrect, and reconcile your life back to God and His original purpose for your life.

However, after your spirit has been made new by God through the Holy Spirit, you are responsible for renewing you own mind so that you can begin to properly conceptualize the kingdom.

This is the primary reason Jesus emphasized the importance of striving to enter into the kingdom, which is God's way of doing and being.

Matthew 6:33 says, "Aim at and strive after first of all His Kingdom and His righteousness (his way of doing and being right)."

God wants to partner with us in the "dominion" mandate He established with us in the beginning. We live in a dispensation wherein it is important for kingdom citizens to know that we don't have to attempt our endeavors in our own strength nor do we have to depend upon our gifts alone. *Jesus depended on the Holy Spirit!*

We all want to succeed; however, there are some *advantages* that we gain as kingdom citizens in our pursuits when we understand the *right concept* of *kingdom*.

## *Does your "thinking" reflect God's?*

This is a pertinent question because if it does, you will begin to learn to work *smarter*—not harder—and live less stressfully! Jesus said, "His yoke is *easy* and His burden *light*."

Multitudes of *kingdom* people are not *cultured* to "think" appropriately; so our life applications are inappropriate for achievement, accomplishment, and advancement. Life on earth is designed to function by laws that demand that proper concept be given premium importance.

The primary reason "mind renewal" is important is because if an individual's *concept* is wrong, their approach will be wrong.

Heaven's purpose for colonizing the earth is to *extend* the *influence* of the kingdom throughout the world, which means the entire world is our target. The responsibility of the people of the *colony* is to reflect the norms, values, standards, beliefs, convictions, and behaviors of the kingdom.

Herein, the *greatest faculty* God gave Adam was the *ability* to *think*.

He gave Noah a vision, but Noah had to think his way to constructing the ark. Man was made to *imagine*!

Notice Genesis 5:1–2 AMP:

> This is the book (the written record, the history) of the generations of [the descendants of] Adam. When God created man, He made him in the likeness of God [not physical, but a spiritual personality and moral likeness]. He created them male and female, and blessed them and named them Mankind at the time they were created.

We are supposed to *think* and *grow* and *increase* and *multiply* in every area of our lives.

In light of this, each of us should demand of ourselves an allotted amount of time to engage effective thinking applications.

# Types of *Effective Thinking*

In 1967, the term *lateral thinking* was made known and disseminated by Edward de Bono.

Lateral thinking is a manner of solving problems using an indirect and creative approach through reasoning that is not immediately obvious. It involves ideas that may not be obtainable using only traditional step-by-step logic lines of rational.

To explain this thinking, Bono mentioned the "Judgment of Solomon" as an example, where King Solomon resolves a dispute over the parentage of a child by calling for the child to be cut in half and making his judgment according to the reactions that this order receives.

He also links lateral thinking with humor, arguing there's a switchover from a familiar pattern to a new unexpected one. It is this moment of surprise, generating laughter and new insight, which facilitates the ability to see a different thought pattern that initially was not obvious.

According to Edward de Bono, lateral thinking deliberately distances itself from the standard perception of creativity as "vertical" logic (the classic method for problem-solving).

To understand lateral thinking, it is necessary to compare lateral thinking and critical thinking. Critical thinking is primarily concerned with judging the true value of statements and seeking errors, while lateral thinking is more concerned with the "movement value" of statements and ideas. A person uses lateral thinking to move from one known idea to creating new ideas. In order to effectively accomplish this, Edward de Bono defines four types of thinking tools:

1. Idea-generating tools intended to break current thinking patterns—routine patterns, the status quo
2. Focus tools intended to broaden where to search for new ideas
3. Harvest tools intended to ensure more value is received from idea generating output
4. Treatment tools that promote consideration of real-world constraints, resources, and support

## *Random-entry idea-generating tool*

In this approach, the thinker chooses an object at random or a noun from a dictionary and associates it with the area they are thinking about. De Bono gives the example of the randomly chosen word *nose* being applied to an office photocopier, leading to the idea that the copier could produce a lavender smell when it was low on paper to alert staff.

## *Provocation idea-generating tool*

A provocation is a statement that we know is wrong or impossible but is used to create new ideas. Bono gives an example of considering river pollution. To set up the provocation he said, "the factory is downstream of itself." This leads to the idea of forcing a factory to take its water input from a point downstream of its output, an idea that later became law in some countries. Provocations can be set up by the use of any of the provocation techniques—wishful thinking, exaggeration, reversal, escape, distortion, or arising. The thinker creates a list of provocations and then uses the most outlandish ones to move their thinking forward to new ideas.

# GREAT THINKING

## *Movement techniques*

One can move from a provocation to a new idea by the following methods: extract a principle, focus on the difference, moment to moment, positive aspects, special circumstances.

## *Challenge idea-generating tool*

A tool that is designed to ask the question "Why?" in a non-threatening way: why something exists, why it is done the way it is. The result is a very clear understanding of "Why?" which naturally leads to fresh new ideas. The goal is to be able to challenge anything at all, not just items that are problems. For example, one could challenge the handles on coffee cups. The reason for the handle seems to be that the cup is often too hot to hold directly. Perhaps coffee cups could be made with insulated finger grips, or there could be separate coffee-cup holders similar to beer holders, or coffee shouldn't be so hot in the first place.

Jesus often challenged the methods and ways of the religious traditions of His day. Notice:

> As Jesus was leaving, He saw a tax collector named Matthew sitting at the place for paying taxes. Jesus said to him, "Follow me." Matthew got up and went with him. Later, Jesus and His disciples were having dinner at Matthew's house. Many tax collectors and other sinners were also there. Some Pharisees asked Jesus' disciples, "Why does your teacher eat with tax collectors and other sinners?" Jesus heard them and answered, "Healthy people don't need a doctor, but sick people do. Go and learn what the Scriptures mean when they say, 'Instead of offering sacrifices to me, I want you to be merciful to others.' I didn't come to invite good people to be my followers. I came to invite sinners." (Matthew 9:9–13)

This prompted some people to ask Him about fasting, notice His response.

> Some followers of John the Baptist came and asked Jesus, "Why do we and the Pharisees often go without eating, while your disciples never do?" Jesus answered: The friends of a bridegroom aren't sad while he is still with them. But the time will come when he will be taken from them. Then they will go without eating. No one uses a new piece of cloth to patch old clothes. The patch would shrink and tear a bigger hole. No one pours new wine into old wineskins. The wine would swell and burst the old skins. Then the wine would be lost, and the skins would be ruined. New wine must be put into new wineskins. Both the skins and the wine will then be safe. (Matthew 9:14–17 CEV)

Clearly Jesus used statements and staged events of provocation that religious groups thought were wrong or impossible to create new ideas. Notice how He used provocations set up by the techniques of wishful thinking, escape, reversal, distortion, or arising.

In His prudential wisdom, these accounts demonstrate how He created provocations and then used the most outlandish ones to move their thinking forward to new ideas.

The technique He used to move those stuck in traditional thinking and behaviors was methodically designed to move them from a provocation to a new idea by extracting a principle, focusing their attention on the difference, moment to moment, demanding them to observe the positive aspects and special circumstances.

The plan was to provoke them to ask the question "Why?" in a nonthreatening way: why something exists, why it is done the way it is. The result was a very clear understanding of "Why?" which naturally led to fresh new ideas.

The goal is to be able to challenge anything at all, not just items and issues, which are problems.

## Concept fan idea-generating tool

Ideas carry out concepts. This tool systematically expands the range and number of concepts in order to end up with a very broad range of ideas to consider.

Now, before I conclude, let's talk about…

# Overcoming Your "I *Can't*" Mindset

This part of the discussion is extremely important to me mainly because there are some obvious things that are discernible and self-evident and there are subliminal things that are hidden and concealed within us, both of which must be successfully exposed and dealt with if one is to experience wholesome and lasting change.

In order to avoid the miscalculation of exposing a problem but not adequately resolving it, I set aside time to think and meditate intensely and retrospectively about the hurdles I initially encountered while attempting to *change* into a more complete person without offending God's purpose for my life. I'm stating it this way because before I can adequately address change from an immense perspective as a pastor, I need to clarify the confusion between the doctrine of salvation and sanctification. Improper definitions of these two processes promotes tremendous infighting and confusion especially among religious, self-righteous individuals.

## *Remembering the early stages*

Once my mind was set to begin the process of change, I encountered multiple distractions and discouraging challenges immediately. Suddenly there were even challenges to begin. These challenges arose from several areas of my life that were neglected without discipline and some areas that were never given serious attention, which is another reason this is a very important part of the discussion for me.

Above all these factors, I grew up during the sixties and seventies when religion was considerably different than today. And I was very religious and dedicated to the Bible teachings and the beliefs of my denomination.

Back then the denominational lines were clear and distinct. If your church members, deacons, and pastors said, "We don't practice or believe *that* in our denomination." It simply meant two things. Don't bring *that* practice here, or be careful how you fellowship with those who do.

I mentioned this because even though I tried to hold fast and endure our church denominational stance against the supernatural, miracles, healing, deliverance from demons, speaking in tongues, prophets, prophesy, and revelation, it was actually easier to remember what we didn't believe than what we did.

While trying to live within the denominational teaching, I started suffering physically in a way that made me desperate to know the *truth* in context. It was especially important for me to gain a personal relationship with God through His Word.

Although I was designated as one of the lead Sunday school and Bible study teachers at a young age, many of the lessons seemed to fall short of scriptural confirmations without excluding certain passages in order to uphold our religious priorities and traditions.

It was in my early teens that I started to experience constant breakouts of skin rashes, extreme eczema, and whole-body swelling that would keep me from wearing any garments of color for weeks. Sometimes the itching and pain would be so severe that only sleep would relieve me temporarily.

I never will forget the embarrassing feelings that accompanied my physical appearance during these frequent breakouts, especially around my peers and classmates. My skin would peel severely, and large scales that would shave the hairs from my arms and legs would leave me looking for a place to hide.

I couldn't use any deodorant soaps, underarm deodorants, colognes, or powders, nor could I wear anything washed in those products.

Sometimes my ears, nose contour, neck, underarms, waistline, feet, and ankles looked as if they were rotting away.

I stayed home from school many days during the ages of twelve to fifteen or grades 6 to 9. If I needed to attend school for testing, Mom would wrap my neck, armpits, and beltline with tissue over cornmeal.

I *grew tired* of my physical discomforts and needed relief beyond my doctors' exams and prescriptions. So I began visiting revivals and conferences outside my denomination.

Around the same time, I met a very honorable man name Henry Cook, a Baptist pastor who believed that the Scriptures were clear about healing and all the other issues I mentioned. Henry actually became my first spiritual mentor, and I considered him as one of the best teachers I'd ever studied with. He was very thorough in the Scriptures and had a genuine sincerity unmatched by many. His humility was so anointed and consistent that often his silence would rule environments. We soon became the best of friends and started a Bible study class together.

One day during worship service, Henry anointed my head and prayed for my healing. After thoroughly examining the Scriptures during the lesson before prayer, I was convinced that God had healed me because we asked Him according to His Word in Jesus's name. Although nothing appeared different within the next few days, I was confident.

While waiting for confirmation, my consistent prayer life, scriptural meditation, and daily devotionals started.

Concurrently, vision, dreams, and encounters from the spirit world became very frequent.

A big part of the lesson was centered around the Joshua 1:8 concept and the need to *renew our minds* in keeping with Romans 12:1–3.

One morning, I was up early for devotion when I heard a voice say, "Have you noticed your skin is clear and smooth?"

Immediately I rushed to the bathroom mirror and confirmed that my body was free from the appearance of any patch spotting or indications of severe rashes although I had gone several days without itching or applying calamine lotion and hydrocortisone cream. We were so entrenched in our daily Bible studies that my healing became a nonissue. My main focus became mind renewal and visualizing myself as the Scriptures suggested.

Until now, I'm not certain what exact day my actual healing occurred, but it was the first time I'd experienced total healing without any medications or doctor's input. After visiting Dr. Eve's office on a follow-up visit, he replied after the exams, "Hmm, Finace, I can't be sure of what happened, but it's all gone. So let's hope for the best that it never comes back."

Not only did I overcome the detriment of false doctrines; but I gained a tremendously vibrant relationship with God, a great friend in Pastor H. G. Cook, and the actual evidence of a supernaturally healed body by the power of God.

These two verses were vital:

> But as many as received him, to them gave he *power* to *become* the sons of God, even to them that *believe* on *his* name. (John *1:12*)

> I can do *all* things through *Christ* which strengtheneth me. (Philippians *4:13* KJV)

Most people want something more in life. They want to do more and be more. They say, "I wish I could do that," but then immediately this wish is followed by the words "but I can't."

I learned that before I could do more, I needed to acknowledge that my former limitations were the result of my limited self-image.

Although I wanted to do more and see myself in a different way, my ignorance, wrong attitudes, and bad habits were real hurdles to contend with daily.

Like others, I wished I could do certain things, but then immediately my wish would be followed by the words "I can't."

Using God's words to inculcate my mind to Christ-centered living, I was able to refocus my thoughts upon my new image, and I eventually discovered that through His power in me, I *can*!

In other words, I can actually overcome sickness, disease, bad habits, sinful practices, mental challenges, nonproductive behaviors, and physical limitations.

Moses learned that God was able to accomplish great things through him without moving his limitations! This is because *He* will be with you and inside you!

Anyone can achieve their goals and dreams. Anyone can be or do more. History is replete with people who made the so-called impossible possible.

Many did it by tapping into the source of all power—the Spirit of Christ within.

That same spirit *within you* is designed to initiate God's plans *through you* by partnering *with you* through your intentional thinking.

The way you think and feel daily will dictate your reality through the laws and principles that generate and govern life.

Even with God's power inside you, if you say to yourself, "I can't," then this will be the *reality* you will continue to experience.

If, on the other hand, you say, "I *can*," you will experience an "*I can*" reality.

The law of cause and effect says whatever you give your energy to and what you focus on intentionally will always manifest in the physical world.

*The mind is energy, and it generates energy.* Whatever has the most energy in the nonconscious mind reflects what we've spent the most time thinking about. In other words, whatever we think about the most grows because we're giving it energy. Just like a plant needs water to grow, a thought needs energy to grow.

You may be wondering, *How do thoughts have energy?*

Thoughts are real things. And like all real things, they generate energy: little packets of energy called photons, which are the fundamental particles of light. Albert Einstein discovered this law (photoelectric effect) and won the 1921 Nobel Prize in physics for his work.

Though all of us have experienced photons in many ways, perhaps you've never thought of them in relation to your thoughts, so let me give you an example. You're watching someone bullying people. Suddenly you find yourself almost taking a step back, and you feel disturbed. It's almost as if the person is throwing something at you. What you're experiencing is the toxic energy from that person's thoughts—and it's real.

Mental energy sucks others in. Think of hanging out with someone who is constantly depressed or negative and how you feel around them.

Fear breeds fear. The fearful mind generates fearful probabilities. The depressed mind generates depressing possibilities. But the same can be said for the positive. The excited mind generates exciting possibilities. The joyful mind generates joyful possibilities. And the list goes on. We are what we think, and what we think about most will grow.

Pay attention to the energy you're taking in. That's why we need to be discerning about who we connect with and who we listen to. We can quite literally enhance or damage one another.

When we inadvertently allow others to fill our minds with their thinking, we're at their mercy.

The energy from people's thoughts is real, and we need to protect ourselves from it if it's negative or grab it with both hands if it's positive.

Thoughts and ideas from other people—including what we hear, read, and watch—have the potential to exert a controlling influence over our thinking, feeling, and choosing, if we let them.

Bottom line, what we're doing with our minds, our words, our attitudes, and our beliefs affects the people around us. Have you ever had anyone tell you there's a black cloud hanging over you and it's affecting them? Or that you're creating a toxic work environment by letting your stress affect everyone in the office? There's real energy being emitted from your thoughts and affecting others.

Fear of failure is a ghost designed to stop you from moving toward experiencing the enrichment power and ability of Christ in you which requires confidence, courage, and strength.

The fainthearted hardly ever experience the dynamo power of God's grace because of the ghostly appearance of obstacles and hurdles to their natural mind and senses.

## FINACE BUSH

You are *one*-of-a-*kind*, which indicates you are unique, exclusive, rare, and generis; and no one on the planet can think and feel like you, especially if you tap into your passion and extraordinary genius. When you do, you will tap into a power that speeds up the manifestation process.

A poem written by James T. Moore exposes the potential power you possess.

> There is only one you, you are truly
> *Unique*
> One And Only You
> Every single blade of grass,
> And every flake of snow—
> Is just a wee bit different...
> There's no two alike, you know.
> From something small, like grains of sand,
> To each gigantic star
> All were made with *this* in mind:
> To be just what they are!
> How foolish then, to imitate—
> How useless to pretend!
> Since each of us comes from a *mind*
> Whose ideas never end.
> There'll only be just *one* of *me*
> To show what I can do—
> And you should likewise feel very proud,
> There's only *one* of *you*.
> That is where it all starts
> With you, a wonderful
> unlimited human being.
> (James T. Moore)

Now let's look at some of the hurdles you've overcome but failed to review in a way that will encourage your *best try*!

# GREAT THINKING

*Why you can!*

You may not be accustomed to looking back through your past for positive affirmations of growth and development, but a brief review will help you see how you've overcome many obstacles to growth. You simply can do things now that you couldn't before.

As a baby, you didn't know how to eat, walk, nor bathe—now you do. The food, floor, or water never changed: you did. Now you can read, but when you were younger, you couldn't. The English language never changed: you did.

At one time, T. D. Jakes didn't know how to run a mega-ministry, but then he did—big-time. Jakes has generated one of the most successful mega-ministries in the world—the Potters House. The ministry world didn't change—Jakes did.

You can do more and be more through the incredible power of your thoughts.

# Manifesting Power through Thinking

Want to learn more about how to use your thoughts to manifest what you want?

In the movie *The Matrix*, actor Keanu Reeves plays the character Neo. He changes the way he perceives himself. He changes the way he thinks about himself. He goes from being a skeptic about his own capabilities to becoming a true believer that even the unthinkable is doable.

Within each of us, there is a "believing Neo"—a super force beyond your wildest dream. It's all about utilizing the power of thought, especially when guided by the Spirit of God that lives within you.

You can become unstoppable if you believe in yourself.

*Anything is possible as long as you truly believe*

We all have the capability to think in a positive matter if we really want to, but way too often, we resort to negative thinking. We tell ourselves we're are not good enough, that we're not able to do this or that.

Unfortunately, many of us grew up with limiting beliefs. We've been told we can't do a certain task or that we can't pursue a certain profession or that we can't be whatever we want.

We've been shaped and influenced by negative statements and sayings from our parents and guardians, kids in school, friends, society, etc. This "shaping" ends up as limiting beliefs stuck in our subconscious mind called strongholds. The apostle Paul addresses these constricting imaginations thoroughly in his second letter to the Corinthians in chapter 10.

The way you perceive and interpret yourself is a result of the belief system you adopted while growing up. It could be a belief that you're not good enough or that you'll never amount to anything or that you'll never do well in sports or that you'll never succeed in relationships and so on.

Back in 1960, Maxwell Maltz wrote the book *Psycho-Cybernetics*, where he talks about the self-image we form growing up.

In it Maltz states that we all carry with us a mental blueprint or picture of ourselves. It has been built up from our own beliefs about ourselves. But most of these beliefs about ourselves have unconsciously been formed from our past experience, our successes and failures, our humiliations, our triumphs, and the way other people have related to us, especially in early childhood.

From all these, we mentally construct a "*self*" (or a picture of a self). Once an idea or a belief about ourselves goes into this picture, it becomes "*true*" as far as we personally are concerned. We do not question its validity but proceed to act upon it just as if it were true.

Maltz goes on to say that all our actions, feelings, behavior—even our abilities—are always consistent with this self-image.

As such, it becomes very important to change your self-image if that image is one of a limiting character of some sort.

The Scriptures are definitive about the fact that you can change your self-image with the power of thought using words of affirmation and inculcated messages.

Our built-in beliefs are powerful. They are powerful in the sense that they dictate our ability to reach our goals, but in fact, they are nothing more than specific neural patterns in your brain. They are thoughts that are so ingrained they have become automatic.

They are not there because they are "the truth." They have simply been handed down from generation to generation. They are there because someone "put them" there.

This part of the discussion is not about faith or religion—it's about your beliefs; your habits of thought; your opinion and attitude about the world around you; and especially your beliefs about you, about your life, and about your prospects for financial fulfillments.

Behavioral science research revealed that by the time you are seventeen years old, you are likely to have heard "No, you can't" an average of 150,000 times. You've heard "Yes, you can" about 5,000 times. That is thirty *no*'s for every *yes*. That makes a *powerful* belief of "I *can't."*

Are you aware that 95–99 percent of *all our behavior is automatic?*

These beliefs are thousands of times stronger than a conscious wish or desire. If you desire something like a new house or getting a new job, it will *not* happen if your *beliefs* are "I can't." The beliefs win every time.

Why?

Because it's your habit of thought (your beliefs), not your desires, that runs your actions.

This is one of the greatest discoveries of the past decade of neurological research. As much as 95–99 percent of all our behavior is automatic. This is why we set goals but don't reach them.

Setting *goals* is a function of the *conscious mind*. Reaching *goals* is a function of the *nonconscious mind*—the *beliefs*.

Belief is also a very essential necessity in God's righteousness. Since belief is mental, it is the single greatest asset your soul has to offer and contribute to your faith, which is spiritual.

Belief makes faith active; faith gives belief substance.

Although beliefs are stagnant alone, when mixed with faith, they gain the substance to become reality by correspondence or right actions. Likewise, although faith is substance and evidence, it may never become physical manifestation without belief.

We live according to our *beliefs*!

In fact, my beliefs are the reason I read the Word of God daily because I constantly need to convince my mind to trust God and to view myself and the world around me from His perspective as Creator of all things.

However, let's pump the brakes and take a moment to be realistic about the constant challenges we face each day in our attempts to remain fervent in our faith practices and our spiritual growth.

# GREAT THINKING

I think it must be understood that everything around us is sense-relative and soul-consumptive. Yes, we are triune or three-part beings. We are spirits with souls that live in bodies. But nature, in and of itself, is progressive and, therefore, constantly demanding our time, talents, and treasures for its maintenance and management.

From the time we're born throughout our growth, our relationships with everyone and everything has initiated exchanges and experiences that forged beliefs apart from the consideration of spirit-life and the essential part it plays in our existence. With this in mind, the average human has never had to struggle or work to believe anything in nature relative to their senses. So to suddenly have an encounter with the spirit world—along with its numerous diverse and conflicting views, vices, virtues, and vulnerabilities—sets the stage for a life of another kind of contentious uncertainty that now demands *change*.

And what change is demanded first? A change in *beliefs*? Thus, the conflict begins.

We are told immediately to offer up our natural selves as a reasonable service and stop conforming to this world with its superficial ways and fashions. Then to complete the demands of this righteous requirement, we must begin the lifetime process of mind renewal. A process that begs for spiritual parents and teachers who may or may not be trustworthy or fully convinced to believe the Scriptures themselves. All these are factors of contention we have to daily overcome even before the distinguished enemy and adversary of our existence is introduced.

Clearly one of Satan's primary aims is to interfere with the proper development of our right or righteous beliefs. This is why reading or hearing the Word of God daily is so essential. "Faith comes by hearing the Word of God" but loses its primary purpose and position in our daily activities whenever hearing is neglected. This constant disruptive, nagging, demanding, and consuming cycle makes me constantly need to pray, read, and meditate on God's words in order to keep my mind convinced to believe and trust God and view myself from His point of view.

Since belief is a product of my mind (soul) and faith is a product of my spirit, I must put a demand on myself to learn to listen to my spirit because God has given me the spirit of faith, but I must believe faith for things I'm hoping God's grace has already provided for me to have and become.

## *To believe a foolish thing requires relationship "trust"*

A trust that demands believing something that stretches our imagination outside or beyond our normal. Herein, it is belief or confident trust that merges with the spirit of faith in us, which ultimately pleases God.

Bishop Carlton Pearson once stated in an interview, "We believe much more than we know because a great deal of what we know was conveyed to us without our personal exposure or experiences. The problem is, we have a hard time believing what stretches our imagination outside our normal."

This statement reminds me of the account written in the Gospel of John about a conversation between Jesus and Nicodemus. Notice how it demonstrated the difficulty Nicodemus had in believing what stretched his imagination outside of his normal.

> There was a man named Nicodemus who was a Pharisee and a Jewish leader. One night he went to Jesus and said, "Rabbi, we know that God has sent you to teach us. You could not work these miracles, unless God were with you." Jesus replied, "I tell you for certain that you must be born from above before you can see God's kingdom!" Nicodemus asked, "How can a grown man ever be born a second time?" Jesus answered: I tell you for certain that before you can get into God's kingdom, you must be born not only by water, but by the Spirit. Humans give life to their children. Yet only God's Spirit can change you into a child of God. Don't be surprised when I say that you must be born from above. Only God's Spirit gives new life. The Spirit is like the wind

that blows wherever it wants to. You can hear the wind, but you don't know where it comes from or where it is going. "How can this be?" Nicodemus asked. Jesus replied: How can you be a teacher of Israel and not know these things? I tell you for certain we know what we are talking about because we have seen it ourselves. But none of you will accept what we say. If you don't *believe* when I talk to you about things on earth, *how* can you possibly Believe if I talk to you about things in heaven? No one has gone up to heaven except the Son of Man, who came down from there. And the Son of Man must be lifted up, just as the metal snake was lifted up by Moses in the desert. Then everyone who is able to *believe* in the Son of Man will have eternal life. (John 3:1–15)

In these fifteen verses, John speaks to us by highlighting the difficulty of Nicodemus believing truth outside of his normal and the uncertainty of accepting the truth without an established relationship with the source, even though Jesus was certainly a credible source.

It is vitally important to not allow yourself to become inflexible about things you believe. After all, *beliefs* are the gateway to heavenly possibilities in your life.

In chapter 20, John again deals primarily with the difficulty many encounter when challenged to believe beyond their normal beliefs. But here he also reveals the denial and the postponement of the supernatural for people who resist believing and trusting God on His terms.

In this account, the incredulity of Thomas gives us an opportunity to view ourselves through his experience when the report about Jesus's resurrection was brought to him by the other disciples. I used this nagging term *incredulity* because it conveys the state of an individual who is unable or unwilling to believe something that they didn't see or experience firsthand.

Let's observe:

> Now Thomas, called the Twin, one of the twelve, was not with them when Jesus came. The other disciples therefore said to him, "We have seen the Lord." So he said to them, "Unless I see in His hands the print of the nails, and put my finger into the print of the nails, and put my hand into His side, *I will not believe.*"

The *incredulity* of Thomas was selected for the purpose of drawing more attention to the crippling effects of doubt and unbelief and how they work together to delay and cancel blessings from God.

The scribes, Pharisees, Sadducees, and the Herodians were notorious for their incredulous practices. Even today, many who profess to know God and the expansiveness of His abounding grace fail to *believe* He's able to exceed their conditions because of their inability to comprehend how He works.

The term *incredulity* denotes unwillingness or inability to believe. It's doubt about the truth of something; it's disbelief. Its main use here is to magnify the posture of many people who are unable or unwilling to believe something that they didn't see or experience firsthand.

When the disciples brought news about Jesus's resurrection to Thomas, who was absent when Jesus appeared, he immediately displayed skepticism and sarcasm.

The righteousness of faith concept requires *belief* before *seeing*!

Here, as a believer you must grow to not need evidence outside of God's Word in order to be convinced to *believe*!

> Jesus said to the father of the lunatic, "*If* you can *believe*, all things are possible to him who *believes.*" (Mark 9:23)

# GREAT THINKING

In this, the possibilities of God are made possible through our believing faith.

God and His Word are one and cannot lie, fail, or return void.

John 1:1 says, "In the beginning was the Word, and the Word was with God, and the Word was God."

Numbers 23:19 says, "God is not a man, that He should lie, nor a son of man, that He should repent. Has He said, and will He not do? Or has He spoken, and will He not make it good?"

> For as the rain comes down, and the snow from heaven, And do not return there, But water the earth, And make it bring forth and bud, That it may give seed to the sower And bread to the eater, So shall My word be that goes forth from My mouth; It shall not return to Me void, But it shall accomplish what I please, And it shall prosper in the thing for which I sent it. (Isaiah 55:10–11)

In order to walk and live by faith, there are some postures and attitudes we must avoid.

*Notice* the objections Thomas raised against the evidence in order to justify himself in his unwillingness to accept it—"Don't tell me that you have seen the Lord alive." You are too swiftly convinced, gullible, and easily deceived; somebody has made fools of you. In other words, Thomas said to them, *you are credulous!*

Isn't this the response we often receive from those who oppose teachings about spiritual things? If we compare Thomas's response with what he said in John 11:16 and 14:5, it makes him appear to be filled with vitriol and bitterness.

Notice what Jesus said in verses 4 and 5: "'And where I go you know, and the way you know.' Thomas saith unto him, Lord, we know not whither thou goest; and how can we know the way?"

To live by *faith*, you must think and act like God is telling the truth even though you have not seen what He said with your natural eyes. Hebrews 11:6 says, "But without faith it is impossible to please him: for he that cometh to God must *believe* that *He* is, and that *He* is a rewarder of them that diligently seek *him*."

Whose lenses are you viewing your situations through? Skeptics' (doubt first)? Pessimists' (see worst first)? Cynics' (questions motives first)? Or optimists' (hope first)?

It's the optimism in *knowing* you can *trust* what the Word of faith says because God said it that moves Him.

*Remember*, Proverbs 3:5 advises to "trust in the LORD with all your heart, And lean not on your own understanding."

Romans 3:3–4 says, "For what if some did not *believe*? shall their unbelief make the faith of God without effect? N*o, absolutely not!*"

The things of God are inconceivable unless the Spirit of God reveals them to us. They are simply foolish; nonsensical; idiotic; and, in many cases, outrageous. This is why *to believe a foolish thing requires a relationship of trust and the indwelling presence of the Holy Spirit.*

*For this reason*, the apostle Paul said in 1 Corinthians 2:9–10, 12, 14 (NKJV),

> But as it is written: "Eye has not seen, nor ear heard, Nor have entered into the heart of man The things which God has prepared for those who love Him." But God has revealed them to us through His Spirit. For the Spirit searches all things, yes, the deep things of God. Now we have received, not the spirit of the world, but the Spirit who is from God, that we might *know* the things that have been freely given to us by God. But the natural man does not receive the things of the Spirit of God, for they are *foolishness* to him; nor can he know them, because they are spiritually discerned.

## GREAT THINKING

Herein, whenever the kingdom is properly pursued as first priority, God's Spirit unveils to us the very thing or things necessary for us to succeed in every situation.

*Convince yourself to believe that with God's help, you can be or have whatever you want in life.*

# About the Author

Pastor, international teacher, speaker, lecturer, motivator, mentor, counselor, author, and entrepreneur, Dr. Finace Bush Jr. began preaching the Gospel at age fourteen. He is founder and president of Crown Christian Church Int, the FBJM, Crown Kingdom Cultural Development Center, MTM, SOY, and CRI, a program featuring twelve initiatives designed to redeem communities by programs and intervention strategies. He also founded MTM, a program designed to mentor and raise boys to men, and SOY, an organization established to "save our youth" from destructive behaviors.

In May 1, 1981, Dr. Bush married Mrs. Denise O. Bush. Born from their union are four children and ten grandchildren.

After receiving his license in 1981, in 1983 to 1985, Dr. Bush was trained and certified in understanding people by the Wilson Learning Institute. In December of 1992, he received his certification in leadership development from the Covey Leadership Center.

He received his degree and honorary doctorate of divinity from St. Thomas Christian College and was ordained as bishop in November 2005.

He is also a gifted and talented artist by trade. He attended the University of Kansas City where he studied art. He later transferred to the Art Institute of Atlanta (Georgia). He accepted his call to preach the Gospel three months short of receiving his associate's degree; however, his gifted artwork has been displayed in galleries and museums all over the country and in Africa, Europe, and Asia. He has nine prominent published works of art.

He established a radio and television ministry, *Revealing of the Enemy Ministries*, which aired on Fox 54, WTHB 1550 AM, and currently airs on WAAW-94.7. *Revealing of the Enemy Ministry* is an evangelistic/outreach ministry committed to reaching the despised, rejected, and desponded by uncovering satanic schemes. In 2010, Dr. Bush traveled to Germany to minister the Gospel and to establish kingdom order throughout Berlin.

In 2000, he founded Community Redemption Initiative (CRI), a nonprofit organization designed to reclaim our cities one community at a time, dealing face-to-face with the needy, hurting, and underprivileged who resort to community destructive measures to survive because they see no other way out.

He is widely known for his intensely impactful seminars and workshops on relationships and spiritual authority because of his anointed ability to inspire hope and set order in ministry. Since he received his ministerial call to preach the Gospel, signs and wonders have followed his ministry. The heart of Bishop Bush Jr. is to see people saved and living prosperous lives through kingdom principles. His vision for Crown Kingdom Center is to plant, establish, and expand the kingdom of God in the hearts of men.

## Public service/accomplishments:

- Founder and senior pastor of Crown Christian Church Int. Center of Aiken
- Board of directors for "Talk to Me, a Listening Ear"
- Executive chair of ACOM
- Member of International Covenant Ministries Dr. Creflo A. Dollar
- Consultant for State of South Carolina Prison Inmates Alcohol and Drug Prevention

Counselor and task team adviser for the Juvenile Affairs of Aiken County Sheriff's Department

Awards and achievements:

Synergy Excellence Award
Achievement of Excellence
Outstanding Artist of the Year
Black Patriot of the Year
Outstanding Pastor of the Year
Outstanding Mentor
Outstanding Athlete
Sportsmanship Award
President of Young Life

Published art:

*Blowing the Trumpet*, "Dizzie Gillispe"
*Praying Man: True Champion* featuring Jack Nicholas
*Safe in My Arms* featuring Felecia Rashad
*The Eagles Soars* featuring Michael Jordan, Larry Bird, Dr. J. Magic Johnson, and Kareem (The original piece was exhibited in the MJ Restaurant in Chicago, Illinois.)
*Both Ends of the Court: Michael Jordan Olympic for the Record Featuring Tiger Woods Winning the Augusta National "Masters"*
*I Have a Dream* featuring Dr. M. L. King
*Nigerian Runners: A Stroll in the Park*
*Mr. Excitement* featuring Ricky Henderson
*To Play the Game* featuring Ken Griffey Jr.
*Nighttime Study*

Dr. Finace Bush Jr. speaking engagements, seminars, and conferences For more information, FBJM 1-803-634-7672, www.fbush.org

Dr. Finace Bush Jr. has written thirty-three books on the following subjects:

## Books on structure:

*The Master Key to Kingdom Success* Vols. 1, 2, and 3
*The SPIRIT of Kingdom Leadership*
*VISION: The Gateway to Destiny* (default vs. design)

## Books on giving:

*The Principle of First Fruits*
*HEARING: The Key to Prosperity and Peace*

## Books on relationships:

*Created to Love but Don't Know How*
*My Relationships Need Defining*
*The Laws and Principles That Govern Relationships*
*The Power of Benevolent Love*
*Healthy Relationships*

## Books on Christian living:

*The LIFE Principle*
*Beliefs: The Gateway to Heavenly Possibilities*
*Tapping Invisible Matter*
*IMPOSING Your FAITH*
*My CHANGE Needs INSISTENCE*
*ORGANIZE YOUR LIFE*
*The Thinking*
*Exchange*
*BOYZ to MEN*
*Discipleship Lessons*
*The PLAN: Personal Life Alignment Navigator*
*Reaching the World for Christ*

5 WAYS TO BRING FORTH LIFE
*The Source of True Life*
*The Stages of Becoming: "Raising Godly Children"*
*Discovering the Leader in YOU*
*The Power of RISK*
*Watch Your Mind*
*The Privilege of Salvation*
*God Is WITH Me*
*7 Duties of Ministers*
*Thirsty for Change*

For your event, Dr. Finace Bush Jr. prefers to

- fly in the afternoon before the meeting;
- be picked up at the airport and driven to the hotel;
- turn in early and stay at a Hilton or equivalent property;
- present for 60–120 minutes sometime between 9:00 a.m. and 9:00 p.m., not during a meal;
- have his books and other resources available for sale;
- use an LCD projector, wireless lavaliere microphone, and audio for his laptop;
- fly back out that same afternoon.

The number of days your seminar or revival or event will last. Also, determine how many nights you wish to have Dr. Bush speak.

## Other options:

Inform Dr. Bush if you have a potential client that needs one-on-one coaching while he's in town. *For more information, contact Melissa Bush, FBJM director, 803-634-7672.*

Printed in the USA
CPSIA information can be obtained
at www.ICGtesting.com
LVHW100744021023
759659LV00001B/4